What people

The Memein̪ ... ᴛ ɪꜱɪɪer

Watson is fast becoming one of the most impressive left analysts of our strange digital era; helping to fill the void left by Mark Fisher's tragic passing. In his new book — part tribute to Fisher, part cultural analysis, part reflections on the Frankfurt school — Watson shows the enduring power of a dialectical approach to capitalist realism and exposes the many ways post-modern neoliberal culture has successfully neutered liberating aesthetics. In the powerful final chapter, Watson rethinks the potential of Frankfurt school critical theory to provide answers, and sketches an inspiring vision of what the acid-left can be. We may not have all the answers, but all of us should be very grateful Watson is on hand to help us ask the right kinds of questions.

Matt McManus, Professor of Politics at Whitman College

In the wake of Trump, the pandemic, as well as notable social democratic electoral losses in the West, Mike Watson is doing something that is much needed; he's asking the right questions. The meme wars have indeed coincided with a perilous fog of confusion and tension among those invested in emancipatory politics, but Watson's analysis of such trends is a luminous source of clarity.

David Stockdale, Nightmare Masterclass podcaster and YouTuber

The continued relevance of Mark Fisher's work is strong evidence of the period of Capitalist Realism we still find ourselves stuck in. Mike Watson builds on this important tradition by directly addressing the memeosphere and social media discourse. Perhaps the emergent "doomerism" of online youth subcultures

contains within it a glimmer of hope for an alternative future beyond neoliberalism.
Joshua Citarella, Artist, Researcher, Twitch Streamer

Watson's fantastic intervention takes on the depressive inertia of a post-covid, data driven society and asks how an important history of philosophy can argue us out of the impasses of contemporary social and political life. Working with a tradition from Benjamin and Marcuse to the late Mark Fisher, Watson shows that a particular form of economic and political theory needs to be combined with his own brand of media studies and pop culture analysis to bolster the causes of the digital Left today. Assessing the defeats of socialist causes over recent years and analysing the digital world of elections and desire, Watson rebuilds a class solidarity from an important history of Marxist theory that can re-invigorate the Left today in the battle against right-wing populism and capitalist media discourse. This ambitious book, taking in everything from conspiracy and memes to economic policy and election campaigns, is a must-read for anyone who wants to join the battle for a better future.
Alfie Bown, Royal Holloway, University of London

The Memeing of Mark Fisher

How the Frankfurt School Foresaw
Capitalist Realism and What To Do
About It

Also by the Author

Can the Left Learn to Meme?, Zero Books,
ISBN: 978-1-78535-723-7

Towards a Conceptual Militancy, Zero Books,
ISBN: 978-1-78099-231-0

The Memeing
of Mark Fisher

How the Frankfurt School Foresaw
Capitalist Realism and What To Do
About It

Mike Watson

Winchester, UK
Washington, USA

JOHN HUNT PUBLISHING

First published by Zero Books, 2022
Zero Books is an imprint of John Hunt Publishing Ltd., No. 3 East St., Alresford,
Hampshire SO24 9EE, UK
office@jhpbooks.com
www.johnhuntpublishing.com
www.zero-books.net

For distributor details and how to order please visit the 'Ordering' section on our website.

Text copyright: Mike Watson 2021

ISBN: 978 1 78904 933 6
978 1 78904 934 3 (ebook)
Library of Congress Control Number: 2021935522

A CIP catalogue record for this book is available from the British Library.

UK: Printed and bound by CPI Group (UK) Ltd, Croydon, CR0 4YY
Printed in North America by CPI GPS partners

We operate a distinctive and ethical publishing philosophy in
all areas of our business, from our global network of authors to
production and worldwide distribution.

Contents

Introduction: Get Well Soon, Society

Spring 2020 to 2021 was the year that did not take place. We witnessed a depression, not economically speaking, but in the psychological sense: a clinical depression of and by society itself.

As sequential covid lockdowns conspired to cancel the majority of public events, consequently disrupting employment for millions of people worldwide, the social and economic sphere entered into a kind of catatonia. Suddenly, all but the wealthiest people found themselves in the position of the working- and under- classes: going nowhere, doing nothing, and with no forecast date of release from these prison-like conditions. At the time of writing, there is no way to know when this will end, although optimistic forecasts indicate that vaccines will soon allow us to return to some level of "normalcy." Though this is little consolation for those who already lived in a kind of catatonic state prior to lockdown, without agency to act, work, socialize, or engage in hobbies. All they'll get to see is other people released from catatonia leaving them behind once again.

Above all, the Covid-19 virus suspended not just space, as it restricted movement to a small zone between one's house and the nearest supermarket. It restricted time as well, leading each day to be a copy of the last. For many people respite only came from the bizarre "covid dreams" which came about not as a result of any exposure to the virus, but from hyperactivity of the subconscious during sleep, due to a lack of stimulus in the waking hours (which had curiously migrated to the night time). It's as if the endless space-time of the irrational sleeping brain was given the task of making up for the restrictions imposed on time and space, not only by lockdown but also by the data economy. In the world of home-working, everything becomes a unit of time that can be broken down into "likes," "views," "follows," etc. Even Zoom conference calls become reducible to efficient and non-efficient facial gestures, productive and counterproductive tones of voice. When the call is finished and one goes to the bathroom the mind wanders, asking "how would this play to the audience/clientele?" Will it ultimately deliver the right audience response, the right data, the desired profit?

Making sense of all this will take years, decades even. As we scrabble about, trying to fathom the world as we emerge from the shock of covid (if not from covid itself), it is natural perhaps that we look backward, to the theories that have helped explain our societies up to this point. In doing this, it is natural to look to another point of collapse and cultural re-emergence — that of the post-war period and in particular the work of the Frankfurt School, the informal name for theorists associated with the independent Institute for Social Research, based in Frankfurt, and founded in 1923. That is, anyhow, my point of departure and the basis of this book, which aims to situate the online culture of the late 2010s to 2020s, both shortly before and during covid, within the framework of the thought of Theodor Adorno, Walter Benjamin, Max Horkheimer, and Herbert Marcuse — the main figures of the Frankfurt School. This is in part as each one of these related yet idiosyncratic thinkers understood the horror of World War Two as somehow linked to the historical process of reification (the making into an object) of social and cultural relations in line with the tendency of capitalism to subjugate nature and humanity to the numerical count (and therefore to profit). Each saw this as a result of the project of the Enlightenment gone awry and suggested remedies by way of, respectively: artistic abstraction (Adorno); the association of constellations of objects and occurrences with which to interpret capitalism (Benjamin); a return to philosophizing (Horkheimer), and a freeing of eros via artistic expression (Marcuse).

In addition to a consideration of the four principal Frankfurt

School theorists (with Adorno and Horkheimer paired together, having co-written the *Dialectic of Enlightenment*) this book refers throughout to the work of Mark Fisher, whose first two volumes — *Capitalist Realism* and *Ghosts of My Life* — were published by Zer0 Books.

Since its publication in 2009, *Capitalist Realism* has never waned in relevance and has arguably gained increased import with regard to the acceleration of post-truthism and the strengthening of a new right-wing politics in the UK, US, Central and Eastern Europe, Italy, and Brazil to name just a few places. While this new strain of the reactionary right emphasizes patriotism and racism, it continues a neoliberal economic framework, demonstrating that certain aspects of the capitalist order are inviolable. The slide to the right is the only form of revolt capital will allow us to have because it both leaves the fundamental social order intact and impedes the rise of the left. For this reason, despite major changes in the political field since Fisher died, shortly before Trump took office, it is possible to say that there is, as Fisher argued, no alternative to capitalism. The left alternatives of Sanders and Corbyn were squarely defeated by their own respective parties, demonstrating that capitalist realism penetrates deep into the political parties traditionally associated with at least tempering capitalism's worst excesses.

Aside from superficial changes in the political spectrum that have served to maintain the status quo, other changes have come about arguably due to a shift in the way we process information and the huge political influence of online media, and methods of utilizing data to influence voters. This has come hand in hand with the deployment of post-truth rhetoric and reasoning (or lack of reasoning), made possible by the redundancy of expertise in the internet era. These are all things that Fisher foresees in some sense in *Capitalist Realism* and it is for this reason that perhaps Fisher and particularly his first book have become the subject of memes within online left communities, at an increasing rate during 2020 and 2021. What is interesting here is how we can imagine Fisher both being inspired by the potential of 2020s era meme production, but also repulsed by it. I say inspired as Fisher himself was always at the forefront of internet technology as a theorist, using its potential to spread left-wing messaging outside academia. Yet at the same time repulsed as Fisher was very keen to point out the negative effect that capitalist realism has on critical thought and the way in which critique is co-opted to capitalist causes. Indeed, the memeing of Mark Fisher himself, which reduces his image or aspects of his thought to meme units within the economy of data exchange, is perhaps both the ultimate irony and the fulfillment of Fisher's theory. There is no alternative, nothing will escape "capitalist realism," not even the book of the same name, which has been memed completely out of context to comi-tragic effect, as will be later discussed.

Above all, this book addresses the central idea of *Capitalist Realism,* choosing to return throughout to that one book of Fisher's, in part as it parallels so closely the Frankfurt School, in part as it has become an iconic meme. That central idea is that capitalism is responsible for mental illness, especially depression. We can see this today in light of the covid lockdowns that have disproportionately affected poor people who are already subject to mental health problems due to environmental, work, and dietary factors. Though, moreover, we see it in a collective stasis brought about by the lockdown in a physical sense, but going far beyond the lockdown itself. It is a kind of sickness of society: the psycho-sociological parallel to years — decades, even — of a depressive economic malaise affecting everyone from the middle class down (and even trapping the elite in the inertia of capital, as everyone is ultimately beholden to the data economy).

Additionally, this book aims to address the depressive inertia of a post-covid, data-driven society in the context of the Frankfurt School and Fisher as one theoretical descendent, given his study of popular culture as a means of countering the depressive effects of capitalism. Beyond this, this book's reference to memes, social media, and digital media in general aims to situate the online left in the context of modernist philosophical aesthetics, positing online content production as a cultural activity that might — as Fisher implores at the end of *Capitalist Realism* — create fissures in the system of capitalist objectification.

However, this is not a book that tries to explain Fisher via the Frankfurt School or vice versa. Neither is it an intro to the Frankfurt School thinkers via recent and current leftist cultural phenomena (memes and Fisher among them). It is above all a "constellation," in the Benjaminian sense of loosely connected cultural and theoretical objects, assembled through flaneur-like forays into the arcades of the internet and the pages of real and electronic books. Many of the ideas were developed in reading groups and online chats, or through the production of memes and montage YouTube videos of varying accomplishments for The Acid Left YouTube, Twitch, insta, and Facebook platforms, which I co-run with poet and painter Adam Ray Adkins. These included reading groups around the works of Adorno and Horkheimer (*Dialectic of Enlightenment*) and Fisher (including all of his finished works and the opening chapter to the unfinished *Acid Communism*). In addition, the ideas in this book have been shaped by conversations with Ben Burgis, Joshua Citarella, Dr James Cooke, Conrad Hamilton, Matt McManus, Eliot Rosenstock, the YouTuber "1Dime," Danny "Badman Massive" Scott, David Stockdale of the Nightmare Masterclass podcast, Valentina Tanni, and Ernesto Vargas, all of whom are involved in the online left and the study of contemporary leftist culture.

As such, this book performs a kind of immanent application of Frankfurt School methods and approaches via study, content production, and digital flaneurism. The findings of this time spent in "digital arcades" are laid out here in six more-or-less standalone chapters, despite collectively pointing in one quite specific direction: namely to an embrace of the possibilities for creative activity yielding moments of life and vibrancy from within an otherwise decaying reality. It is hoped that it might instrumentalize the work of the Frankfurt School in a post-covid world.

Chapter 1 examines why the internet may be failing (clue, *it's the internet*, stupid!).

Chapter 2 applies Walter Benjamin's formula as laid out in the 1930s, whereby an increased democracy of image production and consumption leads to a public hunger for power that is diverted by political elites, to the current political climate.

Chapter 3 examines the phenomenon of QAnon in relation to Adorno and Horkheimer's chapter "Elements of Anti-Semitism" from the *Dialectic of Enlightenment*, pointing to the roots of post-truthism in the human propensity to the projection of paranoia onto the "other." Such objectification as a result of externalized self-loathing arises from basic procedural faults in human "rationality" (which is a misnomer, given that humans proceed from a thoroughgoing irrational standpoint of trying to ward off nature by distancing it with wars, charms, idols, or numbers). Adorno's response involves the mobilization of irrational abstract art to counter the dark irrationality of society, which tends toward xenophobia. However, today, in the post-Brexit and Trump world, we stand on the precipice, trying to avoid a descent into a racialist horror in the manner or magnitude of the holocaust. As such, it might be asked whether we need to make explicit statements in favor of plurality and against nationalism, eschewing Adorno's preference for radically abstract over political artworks.

Chapter 4 looks at the near impossibility of making any statement against capitalism and its worst excesses in the digital age, given the level of sarcasm and flippancy that social media engenders. The idea that there can be no alternative to capitalism — what Fisher termed "capitalist realism" — has become further entrenched by the speed of internet communication, and the demands of its algorithms, which guarantee a co-optation of leftist messaging. In this environment, nothing escapes, not even Fisher himself who has become a subject of mass meme production. Though via Adorno a perverse and maybe useful logic to capitalist realist shitposting is revealed.

Chapter 5 revisits Benjamin, to find him hash-addled and wandering Parisienne arcades in search of some sense among the detritus of industrial capitalism. Examining Benjamin's treatment of flaneurism, it is found that the trash can that is today's internet — strewn with dank memes — might reveal something to us about the nature of capital. Reverse engineering of capitalist realism via an analysis of its digital junk enables a glimpse of capital's conditions and for subsequent possible reconfigurations.

Finally, Chapter 6 considers Adorno's and Marcuse's documented arguments in the late 1960s, when the former called the police on his students in Frankfurt, while the latter became an icon of the protest movement in the US. In doing so it considers Marcuse's predilection for protest as an attempt to claim back human desire, so as to overthrow capitalism's co-optation of eros and deadening of human potential. Along the way, it asks whether the student movements of the 1960s may have ultimately failed and whether we need to mix grassroots protest with Adorno's preference for abstraction. The resulting movement would align with Fisher's suggestion, made in his unfinished book *Acid Communism*, that the twenty-first century left needs a virulent counterculture to help forge a working-class consciousness.

Ultimately this book aims to resolve some of the inner antagonisms of the Frankfurt School, rendering it, via a reading of *Capitalist Realism*, as an incisive theoretical toolbox, rather than a bourgeois exercise in the evasion of genuine revolution via cultural navel-gazing. In doing so it is hoped that the dichotomy between culture/theory and political praxis can be seen as a false one in an age where more and more people have access to the means for theoretical and cultural production and dissemination. Finally, it is urged that the online left seize these means and turn them outward to the streets.

Chapter 1

Burn Down the Internet: Why the Online Left is Failing

In late 2019 Canadian US-based philosopher Matt McManus and I co-wrote an article called *This is How Bernie Wins*.[1] The text acknowledged the struggle Bernie Sanders would face to win the Democrat nomination for the presidential candidacy, particularly given the notion held by many voters that the left stands for attacks on individual independence. We proposed a solution to the now decades-long problem caused by the falsely held idea that the right-wing empowers working-class voters, while the left aims to control them through the nanny state. Namely, that the left matches the right's claim that America be made great again through a focus on individual grit by emphasizing the individual role we can all play in fostering a society managed for the benefit of the many, not the few. This would rise to the challenge of building a sense of purpose for the left that meets the heroic narrative of the right, predicated on the idea of dispelling enemy hordes and individually embodying the fate of the nation or race. Against this, what could be more heroic and necessary than having an individual role in creating the first society that is truly open to races and nations, while giving an opportunity for all to develop their talents through gainful employment? Sanders and Corbyn could even have doubled down on the idea of a bogeyman in the form of the super-rich, or the 1 per cent, as both Sanders and Corbyn did to some degree.

Yet, however compelling the left narrative of a class of underdogs rising up, deposing their overlords, and founding the fairest society known to humankind is, it perennially fails to gain electoral votes. Not least as it is never presented as forthrightly as it might be. This has in the past rightly been attributed to the right-wing outspending the left-wing in terms of media and advertising campaigning as corporate interests donate money in order to protect the neoliberal order. To some extent this remains true today. Though in an age in which anyone can publish texts, images, and videos to potentially huge audiences and in which impassioned leftists of "woke," "tankie," and "democratic-socialist" (post-Corbynista or Bernie Bro) persuasions post constant calls to action, informational posts, and manifestos, the failure of the left to ignite needs further analysis. The tools are there, but what if we don't know how to use them for anything other than fleeting provocation, or — the eternal blight of the left — infighting? And what if the internet is anyhow fundamentally loaded in favor of the right-wing? These questions need asking as the left continues to appropriate right-wing tactics, only to fail perennially. Perhaps it's time to stop sending Doge Dog barking up the wrong tree.

Ever since Trump's 2016 electoral victory the left has seized on a narrative whereby Trump won the electoral college thanks to a few thousand votes cast by disaffected young men turned on to a white supremacist narrative by alt-right meme producers. This story appeals to people thirsty for answers as to how Trump stole the 2016 election on many basic levels: it features hopeless young men working from their bedrooms on readily available hardware, the source of so many moral panics; it explains shadowy practices of the coming-of-age generation to their elders; it excuses Trump as the accidental outcome of a comedically unhinged and yet deadly (considering Charlottesville and the Capitol mob) movement of losers. Finally, and crucially, it's a simple narrative employing everyday elements we are all familiar with, such as social media apps and the singular "meme" unit. However, in the frenzy of articles, news programs, and YouTube analyses of the online right that followed Trump's election, no one really stopped to ask the crucial questions. Not least among them, could anyone attribute with certainty the few thousand votes that gave Trump electoral college victory to the memetic output of the 4Chan and 8Chan community? Moreover, even if they could, does it make any sense to speak of the left emulating an aesthetic approach that is deliberately oriented toward division and stirring antipathy?

Perhaps the clearest case study for a leftist parallel to the alt-right movement came in the form of the "Yang Gang" in late 2019 and early 2020. It's an example that stands as a warning to the left on the perils of going too far down the rabbit hole of political meme trickery. The Yang Gang operated as an unofficial wing of Andrew Yang's campaign for the Democrat nomination though ended up derailing his message by frequently appropriating commonly used right-wing imagery such as the MAGA hat and Pepe the Frog. This made it difficult to understand if the candidate was to the left or right of his party, or indeed ideologically positioned somewhere to the left or center of the Republicans. This situation, in which meme producers distorted the message of a mainstream politician, came about more by chance than by design, as Yang's offer of a $1000 per month universal basic income for all US citizens inspired a young unemployed or underpaid population disillusioned both with the political mainstream and with Trump's presidency. Memes depicted wads of cash, stashes of weed, or Pepe the Frog "diverting" the money toward right-wing causes. This in turn fueled a genuine fear that Yang's campaign was starting to be hijacked by the far-right meme community. Yang eventually dropped out of the Democrat race lacking campaign funds and performing poorly in early Democrat primaries, despite igniting a segment of the internet.

The meme production of the Yang Gang is just one incarnation of "shitposting," which is essentially the practice of producing lo-fi montage images to deliberately disparage or undermine a cause. The tendency in itself has become more of an aesthetic than a political tactic, inspiring a descent into a trash visual culture whereby jokey, low resolution, and glitched productions are seen as inherently more valuable than the serious and polished output of the mainstream media.

As valuable as such approaches may be in undermining the centrist neoliberal political discourse — and Yang certainly fitted the centrist mold — it's unclear exactly who benefits politically from them, unless we see the overturning of centrism as a political aim in itself. Though the last few years have surely demonstrated the folly in overturning the center with no strong leftist option in place to counter the increasingly extremist Republicans or UK Conservatives.

Yang signed up to CNN as a news commentator after he dropped out from the Democrat race signaling a move into the mainstream that the Yang Gang had tried so hard to differentiate him from. Yang himself had done much to cast himself as a new kind of politician: a second-generation Asian and tech-savvy entrepreneur unafraid of radical solutions such as the aforementioned basic income. This mix propelled him into the political mainstream, though it became unclear what he stood for beyond a belief that automation would drive a system of no-strings-attached welfare. Further, his online base of supporters appeared amoral and money-grabbing, making the case for unconditional support for the unemployed in the wake of widespread automation of industry difficult to plead. Above all, Yang's campaign demonstrated that unfettered meme kids can potentially upend mainstream political messages. While this may be cause for triumphalism in some circles, before we make the oft-repeated mistake of envisaging a revolutionary capacity for the meme-o-sphere in its current form, it's worth bearing in mind that the outcome of Yang's campaign was very probably entirely unwitting. That is to say, nobody was vying for a particular outcome of any sort, other than Yang himself and his immediate team wishing him to get as far as possible toward winning the Democrat nomination. Everyone else was in it for the laughs, led by an internet algorithm that drives web traffic as an end in itself.

As the recent Netflix documentary *The Social Dilemma* points out, the internet is hard-wired to exacerbate social antagonisms to get people clicking and generating data. As such, it may radicalize people, but only with a view to keeping them fixated on the internet in angry opposition to their opposite numbers. This in turn generates yet more anger, more clicks, and therefore more saleable information for the data giants.

Seen in this way the already sizable online left is no different to the bigger community of mostly female selfie producers who upload daily videos and pictures on TikTok and Instagram to generate attention and sponsorships for themselves, and clicks for the social media giants. Ultimately, internet corporations don't care what you do, so long as you give them data — and the online left is simply one niche identity that achieves this. For young women uploading selfies, the internet plays on their insecurity at their own appearance. For young leftist meme producers of a similar age, social media companies play on threats made to their identity by right-wing imagery, or by leftists of other factions. None of this builds a coherent left-of-center movement, even if there is a growing communist, socialist, and anarchist presence online.

The lack of coherence within the online left is hardly surprising, given that the owners and shareholders of online social media apps, search engines, and shopping platforms are among the most powerful capitalists of all time. Indeed, we have to assume that the proliferation of online left content on major platforms such as YouTube and the streaming site Twitch is possible precisely because it is conducive to capitalism, a point that fits squarely within Mark Fisher's observations in *Capitalist Realism* regarding the tendency of capitalism to incorporate and blunt the teeth of alternative movements.

As such it is not simply the case that coherent political dialog is difficult via the internet: it is difficult in large part *because of the internet* — at least in its current form. The extent to which this is the result of an inbuilt design system that deters cogent thought processes from emerging can only be guessed at. Perhaps unsurprisingly, there are no public communications by major social media platforms conveying a deliberate attempt to derail intelligent conversation. However, the speed at which internet platforms refresh information to keep users' attention is in itself enough to discourage linear thought or reflection. This is coupled with the fact that internet algorithms, perhaps counterintuitively, do not operate with the sole intention of giving users information that may be useful to them. Rather, they furnish the user with information that will keep them coming back to the internet, and this is not the same thing.

This point often leads us to believe that the platforms we use aren't actually that smart. The attempts of social media companies to hold our attention are often comical, giving cause to believe that algorithms are far from perfect in their mission to apply the detailed knowledge social media companies hold on us. Comic, daft, or simply wrongheaded suggestions and recommendations arrive as banner advertising, emails, or product recommendations for internet users on a daily basis. It is clear, though, that this does not damage the operability and financial viability of large-scale internet players. It may even help it. The arrival of an email suggesting a leftist professor might like to buy, for example, *The Communist Manifesto* from capitalist media giant Amazon, despite already owning three versions and having cited it in numerous online essays, may appear both ironic and incompetent. However, it in no way signals the ineptitude of capitalism, given that it may lead the email recipient to go to Amazon in any case to buy another book they had intended to purchase since yesterday (or some other prior point). It may also lead the recipient to WhatsApp message a friend joking that, "Amazon has again recommended that I buy the Communist Manifesto (insert appropriate emoji)," an act that would itself feed into Facebook's databases.

I want to give three examples here of my own experience online, which occurred in the period shortly before the US presidential election in 2020:

Firstly, upon seeing the by-now familiar *NY Post* headline and image combination conveying that Bin Laden's niece supports Trump and featuring her wearing a MAGA hat opposite an image of her uncle in his familiar headdress and camouflage jacket, I felt immediately compelled to image capture it and post it to insta stories. This, together with a disparaging message, no doubt consolidated my very public anti-Trumpian views for the Facebook-owned algorithm. Though it is what happened while I posted my "story" that is more revealing. Instagram on Android has a function whereby areas of your story are scanned and selected with image recognition software, which redirects you to an online store that takes up a portion of your smartphone window while you're trying to post a story. You can then purchase the suggestion or close it to continue posting your story. The results are often mildly amusing, but mostly plain annoying as pizzas get mistaken for cheesecakes, a Trump doll for a footballer sticker set, etc. In my case, insta basically made the sales pitch, "hey, you too might wanna own that (MAGA) hat that Bin Laden's niece is wearing," breaking practically every rule of sales etiquette: I was offered a clothing item advertising my political nemesis and worn by the right-wing niece of the world's most famous terrorist figure. Though they did, at the least, identify the object correctly.

Days later I was followed on insta by a page called @ qanonofficial. What was oddest about this, aside from it being a little disconcerting (though not that rare) to be followed by an apparently right-wing page, was the fact that they had 20,000 followers but were only following 150 or so people.

For that reason, I felt targeted by a page that mostly featured heinous smears of left politicians and celebrities and obscene conspiracies. I was actually surprised by the aggression of the image and text memes. Only on closer inspection did I begin to suspect it was a spoof account, though one that for many right-wing followers clearly seemed convincing.

Around that same time, I was included in a group chat on insta which comprised several left-sounding insta accounts who had convened to identify and spam right-wing accounts. It seemed — and still seems on reflection — a genuine enough group of young leftists who wanted to spread their message of community and their socialist aspirations, by harassing and insulting their opponents. I confessed to them that I did not know how spamming an @BBC account story on sports with unrelated political news would endear an unsuspecting public to revolutionary communism. I reasoned that it would be better to appeal in some way to political neutrals, instead of bombarding people with aggressive rhetoric. Of course, my approach was unappealing to a young crowd of revolutionary diehards who haven't yet been wisened to the difficulty of *just starting a damn revolution* and I was anyhow at least happy they were trying. Though the makeshift group's policy of spamming right-wing and institutional accounts would likely only contribute to the existing noise that drowns out attempts to formulate solutions to societal problems. At the same time, it would no doubt generate a lot of angry clicks and data for Zuckerberg's corporation.

All three of these scenarios contribute in their own way to derailing any reflective thought process. Though this in itself would not be detrimental. After all, there are modes of thinking other than philosophical reflection and it would be reactionary to assume, as many academics do, that rational thought is superior to the states which produce and are induced by memes and other highly visual internet-based stimuli. However, while there may be forms of thought or emotional and physical states that are equal to rational inquiry in their intensity, the mode of interaction invoked by the above three online "interactions" was invariably one of exasperation.

Unfortunately, leftist activity online fits into the same category of antagonistic signifiers that make up online interaction in general today, and which achieve little else than harangue, harass, and confound. The left internet has unfortunately become one assembly line in a vast factory of irritation in which the principal production unit is contrarianism, as seen in the above examples: You think you're this (a never Trumper) but I'll sell you *this* (MAGA hat); you think I represent this (QAnon), but actually, I'm *this* (anti-QAnon with QAnon characteristics); we are aiming at this (left communitarianism), but really we only achieve *this* (further division). And yet we still ask why the left is failing.

It barely needs saying that if we are to use the internet to build a movement that will challenge the hegemony of major corporations we need to rewire it toward education, organization, and reflection. And to achieve this, we need memes that challenge the breakneck speed that platforms encourage us to browse at. It is for this reason I propose a "slow meme" movement that encourages use of the internet's great resources in a considered way that challenges the data economy while building a community that can also function and meet offline. Precedents for "slow memes" exist in online reading groups, quote memes, and the vaporwave movement, which in its abstraction leads to contemplation. Quote memes are another example, and while the left meme community is often criticized for its overuse of text (often in right-wing memes), a timely quote on an engaging background can go some way to promoting dialog. Beyond this, platforms and initiatives are required to encourage an approach to meme production and reception that uses the positive potential of the internet and its stores of knowledge to promote class consciousness and dialog over the formation of new institutions and worker-owned cooperatives.

While the formation of any such initiative for slow meme production and ensuing discourse would benefit from the use of alternative social media and video platforms such as Diaspora, Mastodon, and DTube, to name a few, there is no reason why the existing platforms cannot be co-opted. Doing so would require that discipline is maintained to resist the tendency of the bigger platforms to engender a contrarian assault on efforts to engage in constructive leftist dialog. Above all, a first phase is needed for communication, signaling that we need to step back from the breakneck aggressive tendencies of the internet as it currently stands and cease emulating right-wing meme trends, the efficacy of which are in any case unproven in the left context. Right-wing meme trends succeeded only because the infrastructure of the internet is inherently right-wing. In and of themselves, alt-right memes only add to a sum-total of confusion and angst that the left would do well to veer away from.

In forging a new path, we have much to learn from historical absurdist and abstract movements such as Dada, Surrealism, Fluxus, Cubism, and Abstract Expressionism, that while facing down heinous right-wing and industrialist capitalist movements, sought answers in reflective works appealing to the subconscious or to some nonsensical abstract language that resisted the rationalist and capitalist injunction to produce ever more stuff, ever quicker. The efficacy of such movements can be seen in attempts to stifle them by totalitarian regimes or in the US government's efforts to co-opt abstraction in the 1950s and 1960s, despite Pollock's communism.

Unfortunately, the absurd visual culture of the avant-garde is being more effectively mimicked, wittingly or not, by the far right, as could be seen in the Capitol protests on January 6, 2021, which aimed to prevent Biden's official ascendency to power. The protests saw an array of delinquents, crackpots, and misfits pour into the Capitol building, before proceeding to take selfies in the offices of elite officials and from the podium of the Congress debate chamber. From the horned self-declared Shaman Jack Angeli to ex-servicewoman Ashli Babbitt — who had left several acerbic ranting videos on Twitter before taking part in the ramshackle coup — to Robert Packer, who sported a "Camp Auschwitz" t-shirt during his trespassing stint, it appeared that the lunatic far-right fringe of the internet had somehow manifested itself at the most "sacred" site of US democracy.

Babbitt was shot dead trying to access the Speaker's Lobby and via that the House of Representatives chamber, demonstrating that this was not simply an exercise in dominating the symbolic order. That is to say, while the far-right clearly asserted dominance over the symbols of power on 6 January, with repercussions that will reverberate for decades, they also signaled — with fatal consequences — their willingness to commit violence against the symbols of democracy to gain power at any cost.

While this will rightly be seen as indicative of a brazenly benign strategy of undermining truth and encouraging QAnon fantasy on the part of the Republican elite, led by Trump, there is a more profound long-term trend underlying the events of January 6. Simply, the increasingly horizontalized diffusion of culture, giving people unprecedented access to images, texts, movies, music, and code, which they can enjoy, reconfigure, parody, and appropriate in their own social media publications (as "content"), has left a great expectancy. Everyone feels they now have the right to consume and relate information and anyone can be an arbiter of "truth." Yet this has led to less, not more, truth, as the only thing that matters is the growth of data and of profit margins for a class of data owners and finance speculators.

For the most part, the profit margins of the super-rich are maintained by heightening the expectancies of the mass via a populism based on patriotism and individualism, such that the desire for power that has been fostered by the internet is channeled into xenophobic, anti-liberal, and anti-socialist movements. In the following chapter, we will see how this process has parallels with the rise of fascism in 1930s Europe. We will also see that the specific nature of new media culture gives the left possibilities like it has never had before.

Chapter 2

The Work of Art in the Age of the Subscription Economy

Ascertaining culture's role in fostering a society that provides opportunity for all requires an assessment of the extent to which art is accessible to the public both as audience and producer. This subject was at the forefront of the work of the Frankfurt School, which from the 1920s mounted a sustained effort to place cultural studies at the center of Marxist scholarship under the official title *Institut für Sozialforschung* (Institute for Social Research). The works of this loose grouping of thinkers (among them Theodor Adorno, Walter Benjamin, Erich Fromm, Max Horkheimer, Leo Löwenthal, Herbert Marcuse, Friedrich Pollock), active in the inter and post-war period, have become a staple of cultural theory in the West over the last 3 decades. Perhaps its most famed text, Benjamin's *The Work of Art in the Age of Mechanical Reproduction* (1935), is worth revisiting not least as it relates so closely to the cultural and political situation we currently live in. In so doing, the purpose of this text is to point to the very real sense that aspects of fascist era history are being alarmingly repeated today in the media rhetoric and policymaking of right-wing populists. Yet at the same time, a reconsideration of Benjamin's text allows us to draw out the essential differences between the media landscape of the 1930s and 2020s. What this signals above all is the continued existence of an unremitting kernel of creative resistance that exists at the heart of a capitalist media system that is still in no way completely beholden to the right-wing.

Benjamin saw a social class relation in the production and consumption of art, linking what he termed the "aura" of a given artwork to the exclusivity of the act of viewing it. However, for Benjamin the increasingly ubiquitous printed copy of the artwork could be used to share the image of the original with the masses, bringing them an experience of art viewing hitherto only available to their social class superiors. As such, anyone could now witness, for example, the form of the Mona Lisa, though this came at the expense of the work's exclusivity, as the reproduced image inevitably suffered a loss in quality in the process of its reproduction. Unfortunately, the colloquial understanding of this essay usually stops here, casting it as a lament over the loss of a romanticized quasi-spiritual aspect to the artwork: the "aura." On the contrary, Benjamin envisaged industrial production as potentially fueling working-class material aspirations, thereby leading to greater egalitarianism, so long as those aspirations weren't thwarted by reactionary forces.

Benjamin argued that the offer of "culture for all" can prove disastrous where there is no coincident shift in material relations. Such a situation can lead ultimately to a frustrated population, open to exploitation by essentially right-wing populists (or in Benjamin's era the fascists who at the time governed over Italy and Germany, with Spain shortly to follow).

To quote the essay:

> The masses have a right to change property relations; Fascism seeks to give them an expression while preserving property. The logical result of Fascism is the introduction of aesthetics into political life.[2]

This porting of aesthetics into political life was witnessed by Benjamin as the fascist governments of the 1930s channeled the public's desire for fair property relations into the cult of the fascist leader: a kind of aestheticization of political life achieved via mass media propaganda and military-style parades. The perceived need to divert the masses in this way was due in part to the promise opened to them by moving image reproduction. As Benjamin argued:

> The newsreel offers everyone the opportunity to rise from passer-by to movie extra. In this way any man might even find himself part of a work of art.[3]

As insignificant as appearing on a newsreel as a passer-by may now seem, this experience potentially opened the role of muse and protagonist — previously reserved for the wealthy and mythic or biblical figures — to anyone. In turn leading to enormous expectations, only subdued by channeling the energy of the mass into an adoration of the nationalist leader, coupled with a scapegoating of racial minorities.

Of course, this has resonances with the way in which billions of people find themselves today to be protagonists of moving and still image media such as YouTube, Twitch, Instagram, Snapchat, TikTok, Twitter, and so on…These platforms offer the possibility — however remote — of an instant rise to fame, as well as potential access to seemingly boundless material wealth. Though the possibility that *anyone* might become famous or rich by no means suggests that *everyone* will, and the stakes inevitably leave many people disappointed.

Nonetheless, the media forms that today encourage ambition in the masses also offer the possibility to become famous and/or wealthy, to an unprecedented extent. Where fame or fortune does not come, there is still the possibility of increased recognisability, together with some level of income resulting from interaction with internet media.

This is to say, simultaneous to the phenomenon of internet fame (and riches) there is a repositioning of the goal posts vis-a-vis fame itself such that while very few people enjoy the fame of, say, Marilyn Monroe or Madonna, a great many people now enjoy some moderate degree of localized fame within their field or on certain internet platforms. This situation has led to the neologism "insta fame" to describe someone who is famous — i.e. has many followers — on the social media platform Instagram. Someone who is insta famous may have millions of followers but be unrecognizable to nearly all passers-by on the street. Though of greater significance to us here are the direct forms of monetization that allow content producers to profit directly from their creative output. Above all, it is worth asking to what extent such platforms offer a redrawing of the property relations which Benjamin saw as unchanging in the 1930s despite the offer of wealth that mass-produced images whetted the appetite of the working class with.

While many such platforms exist, it will suffice here to focus on the streaming platform "Twitch" and the subscription content service "Patreon." Twitch — which grew exponentially during covid lockdown as a streaming site in general but also as a site for left-wing streamers — was established in 2011 as a spinoff of the internet TV streaming service Justin.tv, and was developed for the live streaming of video gaming. Within 3 years Twitch gained around 50 million users prompting Justin.tv to close its services, as its owners focused on the niche video streaming market, which soon became hugely popular while attracting other niche streaming markets.

Fast forward to today and content varies from gameplay to cabaret-like performance, to Jane Fonda style workouts, to dating advice, to art tuition, cosplay, live music, political chat shows, and cookery shows. The platform itself boasts more concurrent viewers than the US-based MSNBC and CNN networks. By early 2020 the average number of concurrent viewers stood at 1.4 million, and by February 2021 at 2.8 million. Additional to these impressive viewing stats, there were crucially 6 million individual live streaming channels operative on Twitch in April 2020 and 9 million by February 2021. The public is en masse becoming the producer of TV media.[4]

The process of live streaming is ultimately an extension of the process begun in 1999 with reality TV shows such as *Big Brother* (which started in the Netherlands), which gave a fly-on-the-wall perspective of ordinary members of the public doing ordinary things. Though in the case of Twitch, the promise of potential fame as a reality TV show participant becomes the possibility to produce and star in your own show. This is hugely significant for the millions of people who would otherwise have no outlet with which to express their creativity, their dramatic skills, or their talent in formulating engaging televisual content. The innovation here, which modifies Benjamin's hypothesis, resides in the ability for the masses to not only enjoy moving image content but to produce and star in it, potentially earning money through subscriptions from viewers.

Patreon, on the other hand, began in 2013 as its founder, musician Jack Conte, sought a solution to the problem that many musicians face: how to monetize their huge online popularity in an era in which listeners are habituated to streaming and downloading for free. Since then it has become a global provider of "membership businesses" for creative practitioners. The model allows people to set monthly subscription rates in return for exclusive artworks, essays, videos, songs, etc., and is used by podcasters, independent publishers, Twitch, and YouTube content producers as a valuable source of supplemental income. As we approach the uncertainty of the post-covid era with inevitable cuts to cultural funding in many regions, such a model may help redefine cultural capital, and "culture" itself.

As a case study, one artist who has made use of both Twitch and Patreon is US-based multimedia practitioner Joshua Citarella. While often displaying his artworks in a gallery setting, Citarella, whose research revolves predominantly around internet culture and its impact on wider society, regularly streams on Twitch, hosting talks with other practitioners and researchers around art and online culture (frequently, memes). On March 24, 2020, just days into the US lockdown, Citarella hosted 16 writers, artists, and academics on his Twitch channel for a conference entitled *Coronacene: What Happens Next?* While the assembled speakers made erudite observations, the format itself perhaps revealed more about the future of the post coronavirus world, at least in the cultural and academic fields.[5]

The streaming of the conference on Twitch allowed for a high level of horizontality, rarely seen in the context of an academic conference. For example, the Twitch chat feature enabled viewers of the conference to write comments in real-time. On popular streams, the chat feature becomes of interest in itself as the audience often has a parallel conversation to that streamed by the host, who sometimes replies directly to comments. In the case of *Coronacene: What Happens Next?* an audience numbering over 1000 was able to comment live using text and emotes. In using technology originally developed for audiences to interact with video gamers, the chat somehow took academia off its pedestal as irreverent comments appeared in the chatbox alongside valid theoretical observations. This can also be seen on independent journalism channel Novara Media's regular live news show *#TyskySour*, broadcast every Monday, Wednesday, and Friday, where thousands of viewers can respond to regular hosts, Michael Walker, Aaron Bastani, and Ash Sarkar.

While such phenomena challenge the rigid hierarchies of academia and journalism, some months prior to the streamed conference Citarella's Patreon offered a model which pointed to an alternative format for research publishing. In early 2020, Citarella published a book of interviews with young political "meme" producers entitled simply *20 Interviews*. The result was a rare overview of the motives of late teens producing extremist political imagery online. The book, commissioned by the digital arts research association Rhizome, was immediately available to Citarella's subscribers at the top rate of $40 per month, and later to all $5+ subscribers as a PDF.

The stakes here are high as services such as Twitch and Patreon cut out the middleman in terms of the publisher, TV producer, gallerist, museum director, and so on. On May 23, 2020, a day-long live event was held on Twitch entitled *Hyperboreal* featuring mainly Finnish musicians streaming to the accompaniment of VJ sets (live mixed visuals) made by artists and organized by creative director/DJ Juhani Oivo. The resulting audiovisual festival is one of many initiatives that have seen artists take to Twitch or other platforms to perform or display work under the Covid-19 lockdown. While *Hyperboreal* was funded by Finnish arts foundation Arctic Pulse, the proliferation of independent art-making initiatives during lockdown signals the possibility of a sea change in the cultural scene, both in terms of funding and format. Significantly, it can bring a group of local producers in a nordic city to an international audience. This is globalized Punk.

On April 13, 2020, the independent Italian initiative *Fare Foresta* (in English "to make a forest"), curated by John Cascone, Arianna Desideri, and Jacopo Natoli, saw tens of people meet up on the teleconferencing platform Zoom and respond to the curators' directions:

> We urge you to participate in the collection of images that will be looped on the screen during the event. The screensavers will be like a large archive-patchwork, a collective unconscious, a visual imagery through which we will populate the forest.

Participants were then asked to gather on Zoom from midday to midnight and make "forest noises" to the accompaniment of earlier looped images, thereby bringing people under lockdown into contact with a collectively imagined "nature."[6]

Though this event itself was not monetized, the creation of such independent online "happenings" alongside the potential for funding from sources such as Patreon and Twitch signals the possibility that artists might simply break free from the art market altogether. To some degree, the promise of riches and independence offered to the public via mass image reproduction in the 1930s is coming to fruition with an unprecedented level of freedom and financial independence offered to creative practitioners, as well as to gamers, meme producers, authors, and amateur models.

While bearing this in mind it should be considered that such platforms do little in themselves to challenge Benjamin's hypothesis as set out in *The Work of Art in the Age of Mechanical Reproduction*. Indeed, the notion that an increased public appetite for wealth and power led by new mediatic forms will lead to the political class diverting the public's attention through populist rhetoric appears to be borne out in very recent history. Bolsonaro, Trump, and Johnson are all clear examples of politicians who came to power by offering "the people" the voice that the public has by now come to believe it deserves, while all the time working against its interests. Each of their movements has appealed to the notion that the public is ready to override the advice of experts, a point made possible as new mediatic forms have increased the individuals' desire to circumvent power structures and gatekeepers to celebrity. Where pre-existing media structures aimed to allow fame to only the chosen few, it is now even possible to become accidentally famous. In this climate, how do you explain to people that they are not worthy of attention and success? Or that their opinions are secondary to those of "experts" or career politicians?

What populist leaders offer is an extension of the notion of fame for all via a removal of academic, scientific, and political experts as the gatekeepers of power. However, this comes at a price, as those same populist leaders remain on the other side of the still impenetrable "glass ceiling," preventing the promise of internet media from developing into genuine political agency.

Nonetheless, despite the similarities between 1930s Europe and the US and Europe of today, we must be quick to appreciate that we are not in the 1930s. Avoidance of the calamity of global war and mass killing requires that we be aware of the unique historical moment we live in and its essential difference from Benjamin's, as much as its similarities.

In maintaining such an awareness, it would be a mistake to disregard the massive differences between the mass media culture that Benjamin wrote about then and the interactive internet culture of today. In order to draw out those differences so as to recuperate the democratic potential of today's media, it may be useful to consider French economist and social theorist Jacques Attali's *Noise: The Political Economy of Music* (1985), in which the author states that, historically speaking, democratizing changes in music production and reception have always precipitated social change.

Attali argues that music has gone through several stages of development from primitive ritualistic cultures to feudal and industrial cultures, terming the last two phases "repetition" and "post-repetition." "Repetition" in essence correlates directly to the period Benjamin referred to in *The Work of Art in the Age of Mechanical Reproduction*:

> ...never before have musicians tried so hard to communicate with their audience, and never before has that communication been so deceiving. Music now seems hardly more than a somewhat clumsy excuse for the self-glorification of musicians and the growth of a new industrial sector.[7]

With "repetition" even the most rebellious popular musical megastars — Kurt Cobain, Johnny Rotten, Jimmy Hendrix — whose influence arguably rivaled that of many democratic politicians, was merely an icon which industrial capital utilized for profit.

In contrast, for Attali the era of "post-repetition" marks a period of new music production beginning in the 1970s and made possible by the development of musical technologies such as electronic synthesizers. Attali saw the music or "noise" that resulted from the use of such technology as no longer tied into an economic system or particular logic of power. The aspect of post-repeating implies freedom from the repetition of recorded music tied to a recording industry, or of songs from sheet music sold by publishers closely linked to orchestras and maestros. Rather, noise began to be made in social or friendship groups for its own purpose. Attali terms this new era of production "composition," describing it in the following way:

> The listener is the operator. Composition, then, beyond the realm of music, calls into question the distinction between worker and consumer, between doing and destroying, a fundamental division of roles in all societies in which usage is defined by a code; to compose is to take pleasure in the instruments, the tools of communication, in use-time and exchange-time as lived and no longer as stockpiled.[8]

Such a description in many ways fits into dreams of the early internet, which came into wide use 20 years after Attali published *Noise: The Political Economy of Music*, giving it an almost prophetic status. The early net was, however, subject to increasing expropriation by corporations, the largest among them being Google, Facebook, and Amazon. The extent to which independent initiatives can exist alongside these companies is open to debate and we must face the contradiction that neither Patreon nor Twitch would have the visibility without Google, and that Amazon bought the latter platform as far back as 2014.

On this last point, it is worth noting that, unless we use VPN networks and anonymous routers to hide our identity and activity online, our every use of the internet — every mouse click — feeds into the capitalist system. As such we find ourselves in a bind as however much we may exist in an era of "composition" our free-flowing creative activity — via memes, YouTube videos, etc — is tightly bound up with data capitalism.

Here Susan Sontag comes to mind, as she argued in her 1973 essay *In Plato's Cave* that the popularity of the tourist snapshot was indicative of the impossibility of escaping industrial and capitalist processes, even when on holiday.[9] Even during their leisure time, the minimally affluent Westerner felt obligated to mechanically document their day, before then paying to have their photographic film processed. In this light, it seems that our fevered attempts to document, to capture, and to communicate our every moment online will always feed into the processes of capitalism, whatever the varied motives.

There is no doubt that we live in a society even more enthralled to capitalism than at the height of industrial modernism when media critique began and that this has been amplified greatly in recent years. If the notion of working all of our waking hours seems by now clichéd it is partly because it is so true to our collective situation as functionaries of the internet. Though this situation may become superseded, as a number of both male and female Twitch streamers, including "Amouranth," "Justaminx," and "Asian Andy," have begun monetizing their sleep, by streaming themselves catching some *Zzzzs* as their audience looks on, occasionally tipping them (Asian Andy having earned $16,000 in one night's sleep in February 2021). This might act as something of a warning to us all: in future, capitalism will profit not only from our every waking hour, but *our every sleeping hour too*. For anyone startled by the unnaturalness of all this, it may be worth taking a step back, going offline a couple of days and nights a week, and taking some time to read some media critique. Yet in so doing, be sure to note the tools we now have at our disposal for self-expression, congregation (at least online), and self-education. For there is a very real sense in which every loss that has been made by the worker and the left since the 1930s is accompanied by a gain. Are we being watched by the apps and devices we use? Yes, but so are our politicians, leading to greater transparency. Are we subject to a constant bombardment of images and information? Yes, but we can also all make and disseminate info and images constantly. Are we constantly making money for the capitalist system? Yes, but we have the tools to monetize our own creative output like never before. The list of simultaneous gains and losses goes on and on. The main thing to hold on to is the fact that the relative accessibility of media, both to users and producers, remains as crucial to the political arena today as in the 1930s. It is up to us to leverage the freedom (however little, however much) we have within the capitalist whole to prevent the slide into tyranny that Benjamin witnessed.

Chapter 3

Adorno and Horkheimer: Elements of QAnon

For Benjamin in the mid-1930s, as for Adorno and Horkheimer writing in the 1940s from their exile in the US, what was at stake was not simply the "freedom" to express oneself and to accumulate wealth on a level playing field. The ability to receive, discuss, and interpret "truth" was in play. The task of reconstructing the process leading to the abandonment of the notion of truth belongs to other studies, as does the definition of "truth" itself. For now, let's say that "truth" as a category is highly contentious and would be essentially thrown into deep question precisely in the name of the equally contentious area of "freedom" by left-leaning postmodern thinkers such as Baudrillard, Foucault, and Lyotard from the end of the 1960s up to the early 2000s. However, for our purposes here it is worth bearing in mind what happens to the notion of truth — so abused by the right-wing in recent years — when it is applied to property relations, as Benjamin discussed in *The Work of Art in the Age of Mechanical Reproduction*. What happens when the truth in question relates directly to the integrity of the property or power of the elite class? Or indeed, what happens when the true ownership of anyone's property is thrown into question?

Clearly, families can be torn apart, communities upended, countries can go to war, leaders can be deposed over the veracity of a claim relating to property or to the rightful occupant of the seat of power. So it'd be inaccurate to say that people increasingly don't believe in truth today, or that it has ever really been contentious as a definition — at least in regard to proprietorship. Trump's contestation of the 2020 US presidential result is one example of how "truth" (if not *the truth*) is strongly invoked by figures in power (or exiting from power). Indeed the "post-truth" tendency that was massively enabled by the Trump administration's endorsement of "alternative facts" is more an attack on processes of due diligence undertaken to assure the veracity of claims on property and power than on truth claims themselves.

Just as Benjamin argued that the populist right in the 1930s diverted people away from aspirations for increased wealth, they also diverted people away from their aspiration for increased knowledge (the two being effectively linked). As stated earlier, this was achieved via propaganda through military-style parades, posters, radio addresses, and so on. Today, it is achieved through a diversion of attention through social media advertising and the infiltration of the far right into Chan image boards and social media memes pages. Though the tendency is essentially the same, leading the elite to try to shut down the impulse toward the attainment of skills that might allow people to challenge power.

This new incarnation of the populist right was heralded with the rise of the alt-right and the heinous racist memes they brought with them. Yet that period now seems remote and crude, like the war cry of Ork hordes clanging pots, compared to QAnon — a phenomenon that is more role player fantasy or real-life whodunnit than mere meme. The alt-right meme fraternity was and is a club of assorted misfits who check-in daily to share basically offensive imagery. Some memesters might be addicted to meme posting and the kick that one gets when a meme goes viral, spending their lives glued to the screen, whereas some might have a busy life as street protestors, or regular Joes working a nine to five, but being an alt-right meme poster is basically an online identity. One can leave it at the margins of a given online platform and go out to meet apolitical friends, the same as an insta famous model who may be unknown in her local grocery store.

The QAnon movement would appear to be psychologically different. Despite the existence of varied mythic, paranoid, or basically speculative assertions of its origins, it appears to have grown up of its own accord from a singular 4Chan post in 2017 written by a shadowy 4Chan user, claiming to be a government agent with Q level security clearance. The original post was deliberately spread around the internet via Reddit and YouTube by a group of three individuals, with numerous social media meme accounts acting as hubs. These memes, while often obscure, encoded to some degree and sprawling in their range and output, tend very broadly to state that the world is run by a shady internationalist neoliberal cabal who practice satanism, child sex trafficking, and the drinking of human blood. Elements of this lowest common denominator conspiracy are traceable to Pizzagate, an online conspiracy that went viral in 2016, linking the Clintons to a satanic pedophile ring that operated out of Comet Ping Pong, a genuine pizzeria in Washington, D.C., which became the subject of hate mail and a gun attack following the allegations. The QAnon variant of this basically archetypal conspiracy builds upon this narrative, adding that Donald Trump is destined to save the US and world from the evil embodied in the neoliberal elite. This will take place as part of "The Storm," an event named after Trump's mysterious allusion to "the calm before the storm" made in 2017 before an assembled press corps that had been told to gather for an announcement but who were instead treated to vagaries about top-level military meetings. The statement was seized upon by "Q" and his (or their) followers who fanned one anothers' imaginations until Trump's words were taken to indicate the impending mass arrests of Deep State actors and cabal leaders from across the liberal and left spectrum. This event, also known as the "Great Awakening," is just one part of a shifting narrative that would appear to speak to people's personal need to believe and even help construct a grand story for our times.[10]

"PrayingMedic," the internet alias for David Hayes, one of YouTube's most fervent and followed unofficial QAnon spokespersons, makes the importance of narrative very clear in a personal blog post entitled "The Coming Global Tsunami":

> It [QAnon] speaks of an intellectual awakening — the awareness by the public to the truth that we've been enslaved in a corrupt political system. But the exposure of the unimaginable depravity of the elites will lead to an increased awareness of our own depravity. Self-awareness of sin is fertile ground for spiritual revival. I believe the long-prophesied spiritual awakening lies on the other side of The Storm.[11]

QAnon has no singular image identity, and is more characterized by slogans such as "#SaveTheChildren" — appropriating the charity of the same name to gain credibility — and memetically spread ideas that supplement the movement's main narrative. By 2018 this sprawling ad hoc story led QAnon to develop a sizable presence at major Trump rallies, while by 2020 it had an international following, which grew further when major news outlets globally began to cover the movement in September 2020, amid fears QAnon could sway the US election. The movement is taken so seriously that the FBI issued a domestic terrorist warning linked to the group as far back as May 2019, and numerous psychologists have been paraded on TV and featured as columnists in newspapers to convey the apparent psychological risks of conspiracy theories.

It is the all-encompassing nature of QAnon that sets it apart from the initially disturbing yet ultimately dated and anyhow limited practice of the alt-right meme kid. While a continuous thread of posts attributed to QAnon maintains some consistency to the conspiracy initially revealed by "Q," the messages were spread by followers, effectively making the QAnon backstory a meme with considerable longevity, adaptability, and fidelity to original posts. This means that while we saw nothing comparable to the alt-right's memetic output in 2016 during the 2020 election, the memetic spread of QAnon has done something that no singular meme or meme movement has managed up to now. A meme is usually looked at in terms of its spread across platforms and as mutated variations of a singular form, always ultimately gauged in terms of number. This makes it easy to identify and count, especially as many memes follow recognized image conventions within the meme community. QAnon, however — like Pizzagate to a lesser degree — spreads into the psyche and lives of its followers, often via relatively niche message boards. It is as if the minds behind alt-right memes got together and plotted out a sequel to the 2016 US Election meme campaign, ratcheting up the element of narrative and the degree of audience participation. This time the memes would add up to a story that required a constant updating of information uploaded to "QDrops" — or dedicated message boards where information would be regularly deposited. Only there would appear to be no minds behind the narrative, or at least it wouldn't matter if there initially had been a plan, because the narrative began to write itself. For the lack of a grand narrative defining our times, the individual and group psyche blighted by mass inequality, covid (and its aftermath), race tensions, and exponential diminishment of our communities, began to write its own story, collectively. Making it impossible to counter. It is as if a late 1990s experiment in online group novel writing got mixed up with the plot of a Black Mirror episode with the result being a perverse narrative that threatens civilization itself.

As Natalie Wynn Parrot (AKA The YouTuber Contrapoints) said, in an interview with Ben Burgis on his "Give Them an Argument" YouTube channel:

This [QAnon] is not grounded in facts and logic to any extent...Their beliefs shift over the months, so there is actually very little consistency, if you look up what QAnon believers think in 2019 versus 2020, the only constants that can be identified are these kinds of outcomes, there's The Great Awakening and there's The Storm where mass arrests will take place and undesirables will be purged and a new dawn for America will rise...is it the case that pedophilic satanists are drinking the adrenaline glands of children at the highest levels of government? Of course, there is no evidence for that, [it is an] imaginative premise inserted to reach the conclusion they want, which is this kind of authoritarian takeover basically...to crackdown on all these protestors. But it serves a function.[12]

This function appears to be dualistic, serving both the elite's need to sidetrack the public from discovering the basic dysfunctionality of capitalism by scapegoating the left, and the public's need for a political narrative to follow in lieu of the one that would make the most sense — i.e. the Marxist analysis that is denied to them by the capitalist mass media.

What is of interest here is the extent to which the Frankfurt School, and particularly Adorno and Horkheimer's analysis of fascist Anti-Semitism and its conspiracies, parallels the growth and root causes of QAnon. While Benjamin witnessed the growth of fascism up close in Europe, Adorno and Horkheimer had been exiled to the US where they continued to be funded by the Institute for Social Research (which Horkheimer directed at the time). Landing in the strange land of Southern California, they were introduced to US liberal democracy which they saw as mirroring European fascism, with the "culture industry" performing the role of state propaganda, devoid of any element of perceived coercion. As a form of surreptitious control, it was particularly effective for its comic and sensuous allure, which enticed people into compliance with conservative values. That sensuousness, the two displaced Germans observed, derived from culture's link to the industrialized economy, as gleaming quasi-artistic products gave capitalism a sense of aesthetic beauty. As a direct reflection of this, art, which might have otherwise resisted the drudgery of capital — whether by providing the conditions for reflection, as Adorno argued, or by encouraging insurrection — has entered into the service of capitalist production. The cultural product, for Adorno and Horkheimer, became indistinguishable from advertising, itself tantamount to propaganda for capitalist democracy. Only the most opaque, dark, and unfathomable artistic productions could escape such forces.

Meanwhile in Germany — where defeat in World War One, followed by a particularly acutely felt economic collapse in 1929 led to the rise of Nazism — that sensuous allure was matched by the gleam of leather boots on the march, and the apparently charismatic charm of the Fuhrer. Only those boots could also be used for stomping on opponents' heads, and the charismatic performance of Herr Hitler all too often gave way to a crazed grimace. This grimace, Adorno and Horkheimer explained, was the pained countenance displayed by people charged with making sense of it all, or putting a veneer, managerial spin, or outright lie on the truth of our meager existence:

But its consequence is the rigid, unmoved visage, culminating, at the end of this age, in the baby faces of the practical men, the politicians, priests, managing directors, racketeers.[13]

The grimace was one of a series of facial expressions or contortions that for Adorno and Horkheimer in the *Dialectic of Enlightenment* express in physical form the difficulty the human subject has in accepting its basic link to nature and the inevitability that it will finish up as lifeless as the ground to which he or she is destined. From the primordial scream in the face of fearful nature, to the laughter in the face of the Culture Industry's products, to the grimace of angst and resignation at our fate and the impossibility of its escape, the fallibility of humanity's attempts to overcome nature is made clear: we cannot, because we are nature. As such, any attempt to try to evade nature by "othering" it through the scapegoating of, for example, Jews, will ultimately fail, however far-reaching and tragic the effects of antisemitism were and are.

For Adorno and Horkheimer, the grimace comes about as our attempt to "other" nature and its decaying effects rebound back upon us, *because we are nature*. The result is immense tension turned inward, as we have seen in the countless videos of Trump supporters, or anti-mask protestors. Their stooped Chad-like muscular forms, minimal gestures, and clenched teeth screams signifying, against all their best efforts, a fundamental emasculation (or perhaps dehumanization).

Adorno and Horkheimer would describe this as a "mimesis" — of nature and death, undertaken to ward off the latter. After all, one of the most fundamental moves in self-defense, played out instinctively from pre-school, involves laying completely still: "playing dead." The armed Trump supporters who protested on the steps of the Michigan State Capitol building against lockdown measures in April 2020, wearing gun belts, padded vests, and combat boots sported the exoskeletal look for precisely this reason: nothing, not covid, not even the national guard can kill an 80kg cockroach holding a semi-automatic. And yet, what is a cockroach if not precisely the horrific dead-man-walking that we all wish to avoid being? As Adorno and Horkheimer argue:

The purpose of the fascist cult of formulae, the ritualized discipline, the uniforms, and the whole allegedly irrational apparatus, is to make possible mimetic behavior. The elaborate symbols proper to every counterrevolutionary movement, the death's heads and masquerades, the barbaric drumming, the monotonous repetition of words and gestures, are so many organized imitations of magical practices, the mimesis of mimesis. The Fuhrer, with his ham-actor's facial expressions and the hysterical charisma turned on with a switch, leads the dance.[14]

Though given that this cultic death's pose is only feigned, as a form of mimesis of death undertaken to ward it off, the grimace-stricken human must eventually find a new form — as a paranoiac. As Adorno and Horkheimer continue:

The unconditional realism of civilized humanity, which culminates in fascism, is a special case of paranoid delusion which depopulates nature and finally nations themselves. In the abyss of uncertainty, which every objectifying act must bridge, paranoia installs itself. Because there is no absolutely compelling argument against materially false judgments, the distorted perception in which they lurk cannot be healed.[15]

This paranoia is expressed as a projection of the individual's weaknesses onto inevitable scapegoats, a position Adorno and Horkheimer felt only too acutely as exiled Jews from Nazi Germany. They witnessed up close the growth of Anti-Semitic conspiracy from hysterical comic book narrative, to murderous political policy, and committed to paper their observations of this tendency and its potential for emulation in the US, so the tragic trajectory of Germany could be avoided.

To be sure, QAnon itself will in all probability dissipate just like Pizzagate did, fading then re-animating as another narrative encompassing satanism, child abuse, and perhaps elements of antisemitism (an element present in many variants of the QAnon narrative). Though even if QAnon itself does not give rise to a regime on a par with Nazism, it is clear that primeval human sentiments have been reawoken, perhaps because the US democratic system of subjugation only barely conceals the blood lust of its people and government. As stated in *Dialectic of Enlightenment*:

> The Jews as a whole are charged with practicing forbidden magic and bloody rituals. Disguised as an accusation, the subliminal craving of the indigenous population to revert to mimetic sacrificial practices is joyously readmitted to their consciousness.[16]

This would certainly be borne out by the history of slavery and the apartheid South, both in their official and lingering residual forms, as well as the constant flow of US military campaigns abroad, and the alarming constancy of public gun massacres. The latter two phenomena can be seen precisely as resulting from the ruling elite's desire to play fast and loose with the truth. They will survive so long as they continue to turn the innate aggression of the US population outward, abroad or at home, so long as it is aimed away from the US elite (a principle effectively carried over to countless other powerful nations, not least the UK).

Adorno and Horkheimer's main argument in *Dialectic of Enlightenment* is that this process will be allowed to take hold in America and elsewhere, so long as the process of demythologization begun in the Enlightenment era is impeded. Indeed, the extent to which the Enlightenment's aims have failed can be seen in the proliferation not only of QAnon but of occult thought and practices online. We have tools of communication and research at our disposal that were unimaginable in Adorno and Horkheimer's time, making mass enlightenment of the public a possibility. Yet too often we use our smartphones as oracles of divination or magic wards for protection, rather than encyclopedias. Aside from the routine of reading and posting to social media, both more frequent than prayer and designed to appeal to some kind of imagined overseer (the Big Other, Lacan's Image of the Father, God, or simply our Facebook "friends"), there is the literal use of internet tech for the purposes of healing, and casting or benefiting from magic.

Leaving aside the possibility of magic existing — for ultimately "magic" often describes phenomena that science cannot yet explain — the pursuit of shortcuts or cheats in time and space leaves open the door to ignorance as regards our material circumstance. That is to say, while workers' rights and magic or spiritual belief are not mutually exclusive, the latter may distract people from the pursuit of material justice. In this sense, the news published across the media in July 2020 that a coven of "baby TikTok witches" had "hexed the moon" was less alarming or funny for its indication of widespread magic belief, and more disturbing for the potential distracting effect magic belief might have on the more pressing task at hand: overthrowing the capitalist elite and saving the planet from environmental catastrophe.

As stated in the New Scientist's "Feedback" column:

> For, after all, we people of science know that the moon cannot be hexed. The moon isn't some primordial reservoir of arcane energy to be used in witchcraft. It is a symbol for mutually antagonistic countries to race towards in an attempt to prove the relative superiority of their way of life. Much more sensible.[17]

While former 2020 independent presidential candidate and spiritual healer Marianne Williamson argued on Twitter — referencing Trump's unleashing of unmarked military officers on Black Lives Matters and anarchist protestors — that:

That's got to be some really drunk or stoned #babywitches if they think that in the midst of a #secretpolice invasion of Portland the best they can do is hex the MOON.[18]

Williamson, who dropped out of the presidential race to back Bernie Sanders, at least distinguished herself as the first presidential candidate to publicly condemn "baby witches" and covert police operations in the same sentence. Though what's really bizarre about her tweet is that nothing about it is delusory. The self-styled baby witches really should have probably been protesting against police tactics rather than trying to cast spells that are apparently impossible even on magical terms.

Indeed, the story around the "hexing of the moon" was notable in part for the derision it stirred in experienced Wiccans who argued that the moon was too powerful to hex, or that such a hex would, in any case, be counterproductive as the moon itself is a component in many spells.

While the Wiccan community has its own reasons for lambasting the "TikTok witches," Adorno saw occultism in general as a kind of residue of historical magic belief, which stubbornly persisted in the modern era due to fundamental irrationalities inherent to capitalism. These include the tendency for people to ascribe special properties or powers to commercial objects (what Marx called "commodity fetishism"), while themselves being reduced to worker-objects. As he argued in *Minima Moralia,* a book of aphorisms written in 1951:

The occultist draws the most extreme conclusion from the fetish-character of the commodity: threateningly objectified labor springs at them from objects in the guise of countless demons.[19]

This tendency, which sees in objects some kind of spirit-form to appeal to or ward off, finds its apex in the bizarre constellations of events, people, and tropes that the conspiracy theorist amalgamates. Seeing a mean spirit at the helm of capitalism, they create an overarching narrative aimed at appeasing or apprehending it and its satanic followers. All the while it never occurs to them to seek to change the mechanisms of capitalism itself.

Fisher identifies this tendency in *Capitalist Realism* as he analyses the film *Children of Men*, which presents a dystopian vision of the UK in 2027. A rapidly aging society blighted by mass infertility sees a population turn to religion as a sole sop to their hopelessness:

Action is pointless; only senseless hope makes sense. Superstition and religion, the first resorts of the helpless, proliferate.[20]

Fisher links *Children of Men* to the feeling, present in our society, that perhaps the time for genuine despair has come. There is no hope of deliverance, there is nothing new that offers some possibility of redemption and there can be no significant improvement given humanity's limited future prospects (in *Children of Men* due to the absence of newborns, yet in *our* reality due to impending climate catastrophe).

In this light, movements such as QAnon can be seen as an attempt to force the "new." Indeed narratives — so essential to human self-perception — are impossible without new moments to propel a story along and give us purpose. QAnon has perhaps been so successful as a viral message because it involves individuals in the construction of its narrative as it unfolds, allowing it to gain traction in the mind of its followers as they feel active in the process of creating a much-needed "story for our times." Ultimately, of course, if the Enlightenment Project had run its full course it would not be necessary to seek solace from our fear of mortality in myths. Yet, as Adorno and Horkheimer argue in *Dialectic of Enlightenment,* rationalization reverts back to mythic thinking due to the innate human tendency to "identify" and control nature and other humans so as to ward off danger. The alternative, "non-identity" thinking, was to be sought in abstract art and music, which resist narration in their thoroughgoing obscurity.

While such artworks would not be liable to lead the electoral victory of genuine leftist political parties across the West, or even a more forthright revolution, Adorno saw abstraction as embodying the opposite tendency to the petty political infighting that itself is based in identity thinking. Yet today we have to ask whether we can place any real hope in abstraction. The fleeting glimpses of reality that Adorno saw in absurdist literature and dissonant music will not likely help us stave off a descent into the depths that Nazi Germany sank in the 1930s and 1940s. Bear in mind, Adorno and Horkheimer were reflecting on a tragedy that had not been averted (and which was ongoing at the time of writing the *Dialectic of Enlightenment*). After World War Two, it was the job of the Frankfurt School to rethink a world that was responsible for the Nazi death camps. As a German Jew returning to his homeland, Adorno was not prepared to support another speculative political gambit that for him would only descend into totalitarianism, a topic discussed in relation to his dialog with Marcuse, in Chapter 6. We, however, stand on the precipice, having recently averted, for now, a Trump dictatorship. There is still much in democratic capitalism to challenge though, as Adorno and Horkheimer saw in 1940s America. In this light, those of us willing to fight the path to socialism, via electoralism or grassroots movements (or likely both), will need narratives.

Chapter 4

The Memeing of Mark Fisher

The sense that society is failing us is felt as much on the left as on the right, and indeed, by every political persuasion falling somewhere in between. Evidence of this can be seen on Instagram and Facebook in the proliferation of "Wojak" (or "feels guy") memes, including "Doomer" and "Doomer Girl." Wojak is a crude digitally drawn line portrait of a bald-headed youngish man, wearing a face that borders between expressionless and melancholic, which first appeared as an image meme on an obscure message board in 2010, before going viral on the subreddit /r/datfeel in 2012. It is from here that the slightly dejected-looking Wojak took on the role of "feels guy," the protagonist of a reaction meme used to express "the feeling when" (or "dat feeling when") a given event, usually negative or embarrassing, takes place.

The Doomer variant of Feels Guy first appeared on the message board 4Chan in 2018. He wears the exact same expression as Wojak, incorporating the same drawn face with the addition of a plain black beanie cap and sweater. These embellishments, together with a cigarette drooping from Doomer's tight lips, conspire to contort his facial expression into a semi-grimace. Like Wojak, Doomer is not obviously politically aligned, though he is sometimes adopted by right or left-wing meme producers, as a blackpilled desperado on the verge of turning toward extremism if only he could fight off his melancholy. Above all, he symbolizes the depressed 20-something male adult, and is frequently depicted as surrounded by short text descriptions of his situation that reinforce his hopelessness: "insomnia"; "self-rolled cigarettes"; "given up on girls"; "high risk for opioid addiction"; "had tinder but too disgusted to use it."

From January 2020 Doomer has been depicted alongside his female counterpart (who first appeared that month on 4Chan), who he is often rejected by, though at times they appear together as proof that "misery loves company." Their exchanges are often portrayed as monosyllabic and almost always convey a depressive awkwardness. This fits the early genesis of Doomer, which saw him accompanying 4Chan threads entirely comprising posts by young men listing their grievances, which include their inability to attract women (or "a traditional wife," as many right-wing posters put it). Doomer has also been joined by Doomer Boy and Doomer Tradwife (a variant of the stay-at-home folksy mum depicted in the Tradwife meme as the ideal partner to young conservative men). These figures, which regularly appear as characters in other meme formats, make variants of Doomer (male, female, boy, etc.) one of the most prevalent meme tropes of the early 2020s, with both a vertical reach (as straight copies of the original Doomer format) and a horizontal one (as variants in form, gender, and age, and, since late 2020, race — with Black Wojaks going viral). The recent proliferation of Doomers of varying age, gender, and orientation is unsurprising given the times we live in. At the time of writing the hashtag #Doomer has 77,500+ posts on Instagram, higher than Wojak with 62,000+, while Doomer Girl has become a popular cosplay character often featuring in insta selfies and drawn fan art. This is unsurprising as contradictions of record-breaking stock market highs and job insecurity, of unprecedented digital connectivity across social media and rising isolation and loneliness, have had an alienating effect on zoomers and younger millennials. Indeed, the covid lockdown and its concomitant rise in unemployment, as well as the inevitable rise of online interaction that lockdown fueled, have heralded a new height for the depressive influence of what Fisher termed "capitalist realism" — the notion that there is no alternative to capitalism and its nullifying effects. The Doomer is a nihilist, a believer in nothing, yet his dejected expression and frequent appeals to Doomer Girl for acceptance (often by attempting to discuss nihilist theory or a blackpilled music phenomenon) signal a will to find purpose, or at least companionship, in a world hostile to both.

We can see this lack of purpose exacerbated today in light of the covid lockdowns that have disproportionately affected poor people, who are already subject to mental health problems due to environmental, work, and dietary factors. Additionally, poor mental health can lead to an increased need for attention to make up for the poor social relations engendered by capitalism. This in turn leads people to seek companionship in online activity, thereby creating a loop as their online activity inevitably isolates them further, while supporting the data economy. This trap, whereby capitalism angers and alienates subjects who then respond with material that is immediately co-opted to that same system, is arguably much worse than when Fisher wrote *Capitalist Realism* (even though it was little over a decade ago). Though what Fisher aimed to convey in *Capitalist Realism* is that it doesn't have to be this way. Or at the least, the sickness caused by capitalism may be necessary or useful to the cure. Somehow, as will be argued here, our depressive refusal to abide capitalism's perversity might lead us away from it. Though only if we fully appreciate the root of the problem in the first place.

For Mark Fisher, writing in *Capitalist Realism* in 2008, the possibility of exiting the stultifying society we live in is all but lost to us. Again, reflecting on the dystopian world envisaged in the film *Children of Men*, Fisher stated:

Children of Men connects with the suspicion that the end has already come, the thought that it could well be the case that the future harbors only reiteration and re-permutation. Could it be that there are no breaks, no "shocks of the new" to come?[21]

This question, asked early on in Chapter 1, is the slim but impactful book's central preoccupation as capitalism's negative effect on mental health is elucidated. Indeed, the lack of "newness" might be seen to link directly with the epidemic of depression and anxiety in late capitalist society (now exacerbated by covid and its lockdowns). The question "Is there anything 'new' anymore?" might be otherwise phrased "Is there anything worth getting out of bed for?", a question familiar to anyone who has ever experienced depression. Capitalism makes us into objects of labor, thereby nullifying meaning as the possibility of vibrancy, of newness is impeded. After all, what that is new can be brought about by unthinking worker-objects or consumers? Given this, refusing to get out from under the blankets is practically a logical adaptation.

From *Capitalist Realism*'s publication in 2009 its relevance has never waned, gaining popularity in the left meme community as a book capable of expressing the madness of our times, as the lack of direction felt by millennials and zoomers meets with the despondency of Gen-Xers left over from unresolved antagonisms arising from the economic crisis of 2007 to 2008 and the earlier "War on Terror." The resulting seething mass of cross-generational angst has for some demographics been wholly unaddressed, and perhaps even exacerbated by a form of "identity politics" pushed by neoliberalism in a bid to placate minorities, women, and gay people, while leaving the economic structure intact. This is not to say that the race, gender, and LGBTQ+ movements are superfluous to the leftist cause right now. They are absolutely fundamental, and have made huge headway in reclaiming control of the human body — which is arguably the fighting ground for socialists and communists as well as the identitarian left. After all, it is the human body that capitalists seek to control in order to drive labor costs down and create surplus value (or, put simply, profit).

However, all too easily complaints about capitalism and

poverty meet with claims that women/ethnic minorities/gay people have it harder than just common-or-garden "poor people." Attempts to overcome this via intersectionality abound yet the polarizing effect of social media means people are inevitably either pigeonholed as "materialist" (including socialists, communists, or anarchists, who all fight among themselves) or "idpol" (i.e. supporters of identity politics, incorporating an array of interests that are themselves fractured).

This is intensely counterproductive when so much of the treatment of, for example, women and ethnic minorities in Western society accords with the history both of Empire and industrialization. The former led to slavery and the latter to the nuclear family and the role of the stay-at-home mother, and then to the sexual objectification of women on an industrial scale. Fisher himself attempted to address the tragedy of the divided online left in his text *Exiting the Vampire Castle*, an essay referenced in Angela Nagle's *Kill all Normies* and Michael Brooks' *Against the Web* (2017 and 2020, Zero Books). As such, it won't be addressed here, except to say that its critique of callout and cancel culture was correct in identifying the depressive psychological effects of online critiques, which make it virtually impossible to maneuver without double-checking if you may offend x, y, or z group (which can include tiny leftist factions even adjacent to your own position). It would appear that the very grievances which lead so many people to express themselves politically online — which amount in short to a lack of agency felt on the part of internet users in their daily life — in turn lead leftists to attack each other instead of the capitalist system. This becomes a vicious circle as the sheer amount of data distributed online raises the stakes in terms of how famous an individual could become by riding the crest of that angst-ridden data wave. Or conversely, how maligned they could become if they are called out for having the "wrong" opinion. The trouble is, it is very hard to choose to be the person riding that wave at any given time, a problem confounded by the fact that one could just as easily (or more probably) become a pariah instead, shunned by various factions of the online left rather than embraced by it.

This all makes the online elaboration of new strategies for overcoming capitalism extremely difficult, never mind the development of new approaches via thoughtful dialog. Of course, we can take immense courage from the popularity of streamed book discussions and debates on YouTube and Twitch, as well as video essays on the former. These activities can be seen as an extension of the tendency that led Fisher to maintain the K-Punk blog. Online theorization, seen so much as a challenge to the conservative practices of academic publishers in the 2000s, has passed over into meme and video activity. The problem is, as indicated above in Chapter 1, these activities are inextricably linked to data capitalism, even influencing their formats. The speed of meme activity and the high turnover of YouTube video production and reception basically impede philosophical reflection. And this may go a long way to explaining why the left is more fragmented than ever in its online incarnation, aside from the gaming-like competitive nature of social media and online video platforms. With regard to the latter point, one can quite literally sense that some online leftists really do want to "win" the online left "game," while a number of smaller "players" enjoy backing a given Breadtuber, for example, to "win" against another. It is not uncommon to see the fans of Destiny, Vaush, Peter Coffin, Angie Speaks, or other B- to A-list online left personas turn on an opponent of their preferred leftist protagonist on Twitter with the brute violence of a lynch mob. The way in which lesser interlocutors can get caught in the crossfire and permanently canceled is enough to make anyone of a slightly nervous disposition wary of engaging on Twitter at all. This goes on in spite of many of the prominent personas of the online left being openly opposed to such behavior, including those mentioned above.

What is interesting here is the way in which we can imagine Fisher both being inspired by the potential of 2020s era meme and video production, but also repulsed by it. Inspired as he himself was at the forefront of internet era technology, using its potential to spread left-wing messaging outside academia, yet repulsed as he was keen to point out the negative effect that capitalist realism has on critical thought and the way in which critique is co-opted to capitalist causes (aside from his aversion to online lynch mobs). The online left is very literally and in so many respects doing the job of the right. So often this is because we mistake the internet as the potential source of the newness — the moments of vibrancy, the "life" — we crave.

Indeed, the following quote from *Capitalist Realism* could have been written about the online left of the late 2010s and early 2020s and the way in which anxiety about visitor numbers (and rarely visitor feedback) impede the process of creating incisive theory. Referring back to *Children of Men* and the sense conveyed in the film that the end days have come:

> Such anxieties tend to result in a bi-polar oscillation: the "weak messianic" hope that there must be something new on the way lapses into the morose conviction that nothing new can ever happen. The focus shifts from the Next Big Thing to the last big thing — how long ago did it happen and just how big was it?[22]

Such anxiety unfortunately lends an absurdity to the left, as it becomes the very thing it ought not to: a kind of sporadically jerking puppet taking on the themes and postures of the day, whimsically and often at odds with itself. This can be seen, for example, in the way that Keir Starmer's Labour Party touted their policy of embracing the British flag and patriotic values in a document leaked in February 2021, urging the left to identify with imperialism, despite its decades-long embrace of "multiculturalism" and "diversity." This example demonstrates how the aim of being "current" puts the left in a tailspin, careering off course while chasing what is new to the detriment of its central message. All the time we chase our tails in this way we end up making money for the data economy, thereby strengthening capitalism, without in any sense challenging capitalism's structure.

This can be seen most comi-tragically in the way in which even Fisher himself has been co-opted as a meme on insta accounts with names such as @fakemarkfisher, @markfisherquotes, @simulacrafisher, or on the Facebook group "Mark Fisher memes for Hauntological Teens," which currently has 10,000+ members. In addition, there are countless individual insta accounts that do not carry Fisher's name yet share content relating to his theory, often bearing the hashtags #markfisher, #capitalistrealism, or #hauntology. The output varies widely, from memes featuring Fisher quotes that might conceivably lead some disillusioned zoomer to pick up one of his books, to unfathomably bad takes, such as the assertion that Fisher was the father of the "incel," or "involuntary celibate" movement of dispossessed lonely and invariably sexist right-wing men, by one sincere Facebook user (spoiler: Fisher certainly was *not*). Other trends include the memeing of made-to-order bed sheets or doormats featuring the *Capitalist Realism* cover (with one meme format featuring a bed replete with *Capitalist Realism* bedsheets and the line, rendered in the classic 'Impact' meme font, "WE FUCKING ON THE FISHER BED TONIGHT"). Apart from being so very odd from the perspective of anyone who recalls Fisher's often-timid demeanor, this meme acts as an unwitting but brilliant swipe at Canadian psychologist Jordan Peterson, famed for telling people to "make their bed" in his book *12 Rules for Life*, published in 2018. This advice has been met with derision from leftists who point out that such self-help advice glosses over the wider material problems of capitalism in favor of small remedial actions that can be taken by individuals. In the case of the Fisher bed, one can neither make it or get in it without being reminded of capitalism as the root cause of our problems.

The memeing of Fisher's theory, book covers, name, or visage in such a cavalier fashion is evidence that twenty-first century capitalism is capable of grotesquely distorting even one of its most forthright and lucid critiques. This is not to say Fisher would be anti-meme, indeed he ran a memetic campaign called "Summer is Coming" for a while in late 2015, based on the notion that hope was around the corner following Corbyn's election as leader of the Labour Party.

He also set up a Facebook page in 2015 called "Boring Dystopia" that aimed to amass images of the banality of late capitalism in the UK. It reached 3000 members before the numbers mysteriously began to plummet. As followers reached zero and the page subsequently disappeared, Fisher finally revealed on his personal profile that he himself had deleted the followers one by one, this apparently being the only way to permanently delete the group.

A common motif on the page was the "crap robot," encompassing images of, for example, broken vending machines. As Fisher explained in an interview with Roisin Kiberd:

> The point is always made that capitalism is efficient, people say "You might not like it, but it works." But Britain is not efficient. Instead it's stuck in a form of frenzied stasis.[23]

The demise of the blog was perhaps fitting, as nothing could be more boring and dystopian than having to delete a page on the dysfunctionality of capitalism due to it being spammed with repetitive viral content. As Fisher explained:

For me the point at which the group started to go downhill was when it became like every other Facebook group. It was just recirculating "content" and sending links, keeping people inside what I would call capitalist cyberspace instead of looking outside at their own environment. It felt like it was reinforcing the condition it was intended to displace.[24]

Fisher also ran a football-oriented blog to coincide with the World Cup of 2010, featuring a number of noteworthy bloggers of the time.[25] All of these ventures showed a propensity toward an almost shitposting (i.e. trashy, poppy, and sometimes pointedly sarcastic) approach that foresaw today's leftist meme culture. Indeed, one can only imagine he'd laugh at the thought of people preparing to specifically perform coitus on a Fisher bed. But he'd laugh like we all do at these memes: at a joke that is simultaneously on us as leftists for realizing how impossible it is to surmount capitalism, and on us again for carrying on trying anyhow with these same jokes providing a "morale" boost that will inevitably take us nowhere. Then who knows what he'd do, given his history of deleting thousands of followers to undo the perversity of the algorithm that can make a page about dysfunctionality dysfunctional on its own terms.

Undoubtedly, the ghoulish reality of a greying Fisher himself becoming a crudely drawn meme character in the Wojak style (the outline of which can be seen on the cover of this book) has brought the internal contradictions of the online left to a new level. The memeing of Mark Fisher himself signals the tendency for capitalism to hollow out all opposition. And yet, somewhere a real-life "Doomer" is sitting on his *Capitalist Realism* bedspread, reading a copy of the homonymous book. As he thumbs the pages, glad that it is not as long as *Das Kapital*, the seeds of a plot embed in his mind that will lead him to play his part in fermenting socialism in the US, UK, Mexico, Italy,

Finland, or wherever (or at least, to try...). For there can be no denying that some small hope persists in spite of — or perhaps *because of* — the mental illness that capitalism causes. Perhaps it takes someone who is so fraught with anxiety that they can delete 3000 followers from their own Facebook page as *it was not displaying the right sort of dysfunctionality,* to also write something as concise, striking, and enduring as *Capitalist Realism.* And if Fisher, in the dark fog of depression, did it then maybe others will emerge into the theoretical and political realm out of the intensely dysfunctional early 2020s.

As saccharine sweet as this hope seems, it is the flipside to the trend that sees the online left descend into a trash visual culture whereby jokey, low resolution, and glitched productions are seen as inherently more valuable than the serious blog essays of the theory blogging era.

In *Minima Moraliai,* Adorno states:

> The pictorial jokes which fill the magazines, are for the most part pointless, empty of meaning...What such pictures act out, in anticipation of their completion by the well-versed observer, is the throwing of all meaning overboard like ballast in the snapshot of the situation, in the unresisting subjugation to the empty hegemony of things.[26]

Yet Adorno could not have known to what extent comic and low-grade images would be turned against the rational order, becoming as dark and abstract as the artists who for him embodied resistance to the order of things: Beckett, Schoenberg, Mahler, Poe. Indeed, the sum of all meme production disregards any sense of logic or civilization, presenting a radically darkened cultural vision not dissimilar to the atonal music or absurd theatre that Adorno favored. The point of Adorno's predilection toward works that had no internal pivotal point around which a narrative would coalesce was to refuse any narrative that would import back into the artwork the fundamental failings of human thought, residing in a tendency to try and control our surroundings. This could only be overcome by a radical embrace of the natural object, of which we are part, but from which we remain basically estranged.

In this sense, "shitposting" — its very name signifying a deliberate "race to the bottom" in terms of aesthetic values — is indicative of a tendency toward cynicism both in meme culture and millennial culture at large. This cynicism means that readily produced popular culture may be able to achieve what Adorno envisaged for high art abstraction in its basic refusal of any discernible value system: it basically exacerbates our discomfort, amplifying our discord with nature until the artifice we create around us comes tumbling down. The impossibility of capturing this moment in any sensible or reasoned way may be why it must come about via experimentations into the fundamentally unknowable and dark realms of cultural expression. It also favors a clumsiness present in Beckett's theatre and in the haplessness of Kafka's Gregor Samsa as he wakes to find he has metamorphosed into a giant bug. As Adorno argues in *Aesthetic Theory*, in a passage one can imagine applying to meme culture:

> The collusion of children with clowns is a collusion with art, which adults drive out of them just as they drive out their collusion with animals...the constellation animal/fool/clown is a fundamental layer of art.[27]

For Adorno, play, clownishness is an adaptation to the rules of a game — of human existence even — that appear fundamentally unreasonable, while art presents a similar refusal to comply with the falsity of society. Today the meme community refuses to play along with a society so false that barely any politician makes a claim to "truth" anymore. The shitpost meme featuring Mark Fisher, his book, or his ideas ultimately confronts this reality, even overturning the modern canons of anti-capitalism in a kind of mock derision that signals, as Fisher well knew, that we have a lot further yet to go until we realize any kind of socialist society.

We don't deserve to be triumphant because we are wholly complicit with the system we despise. We know that minerals for our mobile devices are often mined by slaves on the African continent but are somehow able to countenance this fact. If Adorno saw virtually no hope left in the 1940s to 1960s, what hope can we now have for an escape from capitalism as we are constantly plugged into devices made by slaves that turn our leisure time into productive labor for the data economy? What today can resist the pervasive depression wrought by capitalism's constant demands?

Fisher answers this question at the end of *Capitalist Realism* with a decidedly Adornian response. Namely, if nothing is to be found outside the dark madness of capitalism, the Doomers among us will have to make our sickness into a credible protest movement:

> We must convert widespread mental health problems from medicalized conditions into effective antagonisms. Affective disorders are forms of captured discontent; this disaffection can and must be channeled outwards, directed towards its real cause, Capital.[28]

In this case, it does matter that the online tools which might set us free by giving us a mode of expression are the same ones that feed our depression, as it is precisely out of our depression (or anxiety, or psychosis) that we might find the will to go on. And in going on we may find uses for the internet that challenge the data economy's tendency toward competition.

Of course, Fisher departed us young and at his own hands, and so did Benjamin, but Adorno survived until a heart attack took him at 63, and Marcuse to the age of 81. Above all, their words still inspire, and might help lead us to a new era of solidarity and creativity, if we can see past our own personal advancement online.

Chapter 5

Benjamin and the Digital Flaneur

The "Time Machine" meme, which first appeared in the summer of 2020, features two levels — the upper titled "women with a time machine," the lower "men with a time machine." The woman is typically represented by the Doomer Girl or Trad girl (see Chapter 3 for an explanation of the history of these memes) and the man by the Nordic Gamer meme (featuring a blond bearded nordic man). The meme typically portrays the female meme character going back in time to meet her grandmother or to relay some important information to a famous person to avoid them encountering difficulty. The square-jawed Nordic Gamer tends to travel back into history to try and change events at the macro level by, for example, encountering the CIA prior to November 22, 1963, and telling them that Kennedy will be shot (which, the joke runs, they already know!). The Time Travel meme perhaps became so prevalent in 2020 as it reflected a desire for escape from covid lockdown. Though beyond conveying a desire for release from virtual house imprisonment (or, to be more accurate, house and the nearest supermarket), the meme expresses the degree to which our current conditions in any given time are indebted to the past. Ultimately, we can't change the present without understanding the past. Of course, if a time machine existed, we might be tempted to go back and ask Benjamin and Adorno what they think of today's media culture. We might even push Benjamin to leave on his journey to the French-Spanish border in 1940 just a few days earlier than he did. But history itself is non-malleable and we are left instead in the position of reconfiguring the objects and theories that have been left to us. This was, as it happens, precisely the course of action Benjamin recommended.

Walter Benjamin died at his own hands at the French-Spanish border on September 26, 1940, following news that his route to Portugal and from there to the US had been closed just before he was due to flee the Nazis who had swept through France. This cut short the life of a scholar and aesthetician absolutely committed to highlighting the centrality of culture to the leftist materialist cause. For Benjamin, the cultural object was not so much a lens through which the true conditions of material reality could be apprehended, as was the case for his colleague and mentor Theodor Adorno. Rather, the cultural object was the true face of the economic system once it's machinic mask had been sloughed off. Adorno saw a stirring up of reality through radically abstract works as producing a "shudder" in the viewer or listener that would reveal the unsound bases of capitalist realism itself. Benjamin, on the other hand, aimed to reconstruct reality out of the constituent fragments that capitalist history has produced. Adorno wanted art to mirror and expose capitalist objects so as to reach the truth of our simultaneous link to and estrangement from the natural order, whereas Benjamin wanted to caress and cajole those scattered objects back into a unified whole.

For the latter, constellations of objects taken together can assume a "phantasmagoric" property, interacting with one another in a play about human history that reveals both the present material circumstance and its historical genesis. This fascination with the "phantasmagoria" — a word that Benjamin applied to the quasi-enchanting quality of the Paris Arcades which he sought to document in his last unfinished project — provides the key both to understanding his Marxism and his relevance to cultural inquiry today.

On the former point — his commitment to Marx — Benjamin encountered considerable criticism from Adorno and Horkheimer, his elders at the Frankfurt School who had arranged for him a grant to keep his *Arcades Project* going during the 1930s when funding from his family dried up. *The Arcades Project*, which began as an essay in 1927, was to become a grand textual reconstruction of the conditions of twentieth-century capital that had arisen from nineteenth-century industry. This reconstruction was conducted via a kind of psychogeographical exploration of the "Paris Arcades" — small enclosed streets that were a fundamental part of Parisian commercial life in the nineteenth and early-twentieth centuries. These arcades went hand in hand with flaneurism — the tendency for fashionable middle-class Parisians to wander the streets, half loafing, half exploring the wonders of modernity and the traces of the past.

Undertaking *The Arcades Project* was akin to trying to understand the machinations of today's data capitalism by trawling online shopping pages using a Windows 95 browser. Indeed, the desire to apprehend capital's essence via a revisiting of the architectural constructs of the mid-to-late 1800s has parallels with Mark Fisher's hauntological works *Ghosts of My Life* and the *Weird and the Eerie*, which were presaged in *Capitalist Realism*. "Hauntology" is a term that is owed to Derrida, who referenced the way in which the "Specter of Marxism" haunted Europe even in the late capitalist period of the post-war twentieth century. The term itself is a pun on ontology, the study of being, making hauntology a consideration of the indebtedness of being to the specters of both an unobtainable past and a future that will never arrive. Such a back and forth of history is referenced by Fisher in *Capitalist Realism* to indicate the tragic way in which capitalism forecloses the possibility of history moving on beyond late capitalism itself:

> In his dreadful lassitude and objectless rage, Cobain seemed to give wearied voice to the despondency of the generation that had come after history, whose every move was anticipated, tracked, bought and sold before it had even happened.[29]

The mixture of lassitude and objectless rage conveyed in Cobain's voice was clearly not modeled for effect, yet he was paraded on MTV and countless other TV shows, radio broadcasts, and concert stages precisely as if it was. This is the same tendency that led Fisher himself to become a meme, reducing his theory to caricatured soundbites.

Though aside from capitalism aping our best musicians, theorists, and artists so that they become parodies of themselves, it threatens our very existence as living beings in the fullest and truest sense. Arguably a "life" requires new moments just as a heart cannot only beat once, but must beat constantly for the human body to function. Life without new moments becomes drab and objective, this being effectively Marx's complaint against the alienating effect of repetitive labor. The purpose of what Adorno termed the "culture industry" is to rid from art the capacity to create new and shocking moments that might shake people from their objective complacency as workers whose sole purpose is to produce capital. As Adorno argues in relation to true art, when it can be said to actually exist:

> Scars of damage and disruption are the modern's seal of authenticity; by their means, art desperately negates the closed confines of the ever same; explosion is one of its variants. Anti-traditional energy becomes a voracious vortex.[30]

Written in *Minima Moralia*, a book sub-headed "Reflections from Damaged life," these lines indicate what has been lost to us as the capitalist system appropriates art as mere decoration meant to placate worker subjects so that they remain in their objectified state. Not long after Nirvana's meteoric rise — spanning just 3 years from Nevermind's release to Cobain's death in April 1994 — major record labels stopped pushing bands grown in the garage by angry young guys and gals and started manufacturing bands, or at least carefully screening them to weed out any genuine rebelliousness.

Given the impossibility of incisive artistic sentiment emerging from the culture industry, Adorno, like Benjamin, attempted analyses of estranged cultural forms via fragmentary and polemic texts that aim to reveal their true material conditions. This fascination with media objects and commodities leaves them appearing to be completely estranged from any genuine interaction with the workers' movement, the success of which, according to Marx, would depend on the overthrow of the bourgeois class and the redistribution of its wealth, divvying up its profits on a needs basis.

As Benjamin's paymasters and superiors at the Institute for Social Research, Adorno and Horkheimer criticized Benjamin's Arcades Project precisely for its lack of commitment to Marx. These criticisms, which can be seen in Benjamin's exchange of letters with his superiors at the Institute for Social Research — who lived in the US while Benjamin wrote perilously in Paris — seemed to be taken on board as Benjamin certainly included extensive notes on Marx in the version of *The Arcades Project* that he left to us. It would appear that the unfinished book is a working out of a unified theory of Jewish mysticism, Marxist economics, and modernist critique, using flaneurism as a method. It is valuable precisely for the very real sense that Benjamin was grappling with Marx as he wandered the arcades of Paris with half his mind on Baudelaire's poetry. After all, when is anyone ever reading Marx, or anything, especially today, without half a mind on something else? With Benjamin, this sense of distraction was elevated to a literary — dare one say, theoretical — method. Far from distracting from the root causes of capitalism, this actually serves to incorporate the conditions of capitalism, which interrupts all aspects of daily life, into research as a kind of "immanent" critique. Indeed, if, as Adorno and Benjamin would agree, capitalism inflects all human experience, we have no choice but to conduct critiques of capitalism with an awareness of its intrusion on our thought.

In any case, Adorno, Horkheimer, et al. never themselves managed to unify economics with aesthetics and it is likely that their admonitions that Benjamin needed to read Marx were in part notes to themselves. Ultimately, the truth is that any given scholar is likely to approach the leftist cause from a more materialist or cultural purview, doing little to dislodge the reductive observation that either culture runs downstream from politics, or vice versa. What Benjamin, and to some extent Adorno, aimed to demonstrate was that culture and economics are thoroughly intertwined and not just in the sense that the former is dependent on the latter for subsistence. For Adorno, this revolved in large part around the sedimentation of material history in the artwork as its "truth content." In short, for Adorno the message conveyed in an artwork is dependent on the raw materials and labor process from which it derives (with canvas and oil paint, for example, undergoing a process of labor upon cotton, oil, and pigment as raw natural materials). This means that however autonomous from societal mechanisms an artwork may appear to be in its final form, it will ultimately betray something of the conflictual conditions from which it arose, harking back to the primary conflict between human subject and natural object that underlies human labor. Culture, therefore, is always a material and economic consideration.

For Benjamin material history was not recalled as a datum broken down and conveyed via the vibrating strings of an orchestral instrument that, made of wood and metal, recalls the felling of trees and mining of metals (as for Adorno). Rather, in the Benjaminian "phantasmagoria" — a word recalling a kind of eighteenth-century ghost scene created with shadow and lights — the products of twentieth-century commerce, sold in arcades, assembled from the past a constellation that gave form to the present, thereby reconstructing the history of capitalism as a living model. The commodities in the gleaming nineteenth-century arcade constituted the present as the accumulation of past experience. In this sense, the past was not embedded in culture as a distant cry associated with the primal fear of nature and of our removal from it as human subjects — as Adorno would have it. Rather, our cultural conditions are the accumulation and projection of past conditions playing out in the now as if the debris of the past were alive with us. The crucial point here is far from semantic. Adorno's term "shudder" signals the shock the viewer of art experiences as they relive the primal scream that primitive man voiced at his realization of our separation from nature. Whereas Benjamin's phantasmagoria signals that all of history comprises our experience of the now thereby bringing an immediacy to our interaction both with art and consumer products as if, one could argue, the originary primal scream of our ancestors had not ended but was in fact being perpetually voiced in response to the accumulated debris of history arising from that scream. As Benjamin famously stated in his often quoted description of Paul Klee's print, the *Angelus Novelus*, which Benjamin bought in 1921:

His face is turned toward the past. Where we perceive a chain of events, he sees one single catastrophe which keeps piling wreckage upon wreckage and hurls it in front of his feet. The angel would like to stay, awaken the dead, and make whole what has been smashed. But a storm is blowing from Paradise; it has got caught in his wings with such violence that the angel can no longer close them. The storm irresistibly propels him into the future to which his back is turned, while the pile of debris before him grows skyward. The storm is what we call progress.[31]

The almost cartoon-like "Angel of History" that Klee depicted is portrayed as representing the present moment, facing backward upon the wreckage of the past. The implication is that we proceed not by looking onto a future of boundless possibility that we shape using the knowledge and tools we have accumulated around us. Rather, we look back upon the detritus scattered behind us, receding into a future that will be shaped by our reaction to this accumulation of past experiences. What Benjamin aimed to do was draw constellations from that cultural debris so as to understand how it came about. What was the force that led all history to explode into a configuration of strewn artifacts, as if ravenous hyenas had torn apart the bin liner of human experience? And how to piece it together again?

It is worth considering the "What Vibe do I Give Off?" meme, and the way in which it unwittingly and playfully engages in a form of constellation building in the Benjaminian spirit. As the website knowyourmeme.com states, the What Vibe do I Give Off? meme:

> ...features a variety of typically cursed or unusual images and characters labeled with a number or letter so that a commentator may answer with items they think suits the poster.[32]

The meme format, which was first featured on Facebook in 2020, arranges gaudy objects and items of clothing in rows according to type, so that the top row may feature anime cartoon characters, the next a series of unrelated objects (such as a box of Tampax, a guillotine, a kitsch ornament), the next row some cans of energy drink, and the final row a selection of album covers from trash bands. Whatever configuration of these objects you choose to describe, your vibe will probably be hideous, although there will be "lesser evils" among the possible configurations.

What is significant here is the way in which the accumulated debris of our consumer era points with no difficulty to the absurdity of capitalist society. For sure, these images are chosen to disturb the viewer, though they are for the main part objects or cultural symbols that we could easily come across in the course of a day, either online or in the shopping arcade. The invitation to configure them so as to describe someone's vibe practically invites a reconfiguration of material relations along the lines Benjamin envisaged. The perhaps unwittingly advanced "joke" of the meme resides in part in the fact that we cannot construct a meaningful identity out of the things we see all around us today. Whatever images, objects, and ideas the internet throws at us are largely unpalatable precisely as capitalist society has rendered all experience as meaningless dross. For Benjamin, this thoroughgoing commodification of society gives us no choice but to approach the history of materialism via the sensual apprehensions of objects in juxtapositions that associate freely. In so doing, we may accumulate a wide enough variation to allow us to better understand and thereby unpick capitalism.

This method began as the flow of consciousness text *One Way Street* (1928), a series of fragmented reflections on people and places that Benjamin wrote to be shared with friends. This overlapped with the early *Arcades Project*, leading Benjamin on a hash-fueled, decade-long, cultural geographic mapping of the arcades that would have resulted in a work to rival any of those by his Frankfurt School elders, had it been completed. As it stands, the unfinished *Arcades Project* — the manuscript of which Georges Bataille sequestered in a vault in Bibliotheque Nationale — comprises over 1000 pages. The content, divided into 36 *convolutes*, or "folders," varies from notes on the nineteenth-century Paris Expos — kind of grand fairs of the industrial capitalist epoch — to reflections on the Paris Commune, to records of Benjamin's meandering walks, to reams of quotes and notes on literary figures such as Baudelaire, Fourier, and — under pressure from Adorno and Horkheimer — Marx.

The resulting book of notes is as scattered as history itself, yet clear in its central ambition. Namely, to upend materialism by putting the cart before the horse, having the commodity constitute history and not vice versa. In setting about to achieve this, Benjamin's forays into the arcades of Paris aimed to illuminate the character of capitalism so as to better see and then configure the debris arising from it. Though why do this at all? After all, there seemed something childlike in the obstinacy with which Benjamin desired to invert history. Like an infant who refuses to accept that she or he cannot move objects with willpower alone (as we have all tried). Why would one need to do such a thing, rather than simply letting physics act as it usually does? Though perhaps we truly are receding perpetually and watching history unfold ahead of us.

Benjamin's motivation arguably becomes clearer if one considers *The Work of Art in the Age of Mechanical Reproduction*, written in 1935 during the course of research for *The Arcades Project* and inseparable from its concerns in the writer's mind. As seen here in Chapter 2, the mechanical reproduction essay documented the effects of the most up-to-date cultural technologies — such as magazines, posters, and films — on the material and political reality of 1930s Europe. In so doing, contemporary conditions of cultural consumerism were used to cast light on prior modalities of cultural ownership and their links to the current condition of proprietary ownership. What is crucial here is the way in which a vast proportion of the public came into ownership of cultural goods when their immediate ancestors would rarely have experienced image artifacts at all, other than in churches, state buildings, or at the behest of the wealthy, for their own self-promotion. The accumulation of personal cultural objects — however much filtered and diminished by their mechanical reproduction — allowed people to construct their own histories and form their own aspirations.

It was this that led the fascists to divert people's attention from the true origin of current property relations in their time. This obfuscation was for Benjamin, who held his own personal guilt at being raised in a bourgeois family — while also seeing his own families' wealth wither in World War Two — the principal oppression to overcome. The immediacy of visual reality, available to all, could give people eyes onto the artifacts of history, and with it an insight into the true conditions of capitalism. This being the case, Benjamin aimed to understand early industrial capitalism by retreading the arcades, which were haunted by the powerplay of earlier decades and centuries. In doing so, he could better understand his own era, and perhaps help reconfigure it into a new constellation out of the objects that history had left to him.

Today, looking back over 80 years of mediatic and artistic development, it cannot be doubted that access to visual culture — and with it, literature, current affairs programming, meme production — may all be said to enrich lives. Yet, at the same time, image technologies are in the twenty-first century so inextricably linked to advertising, commerce, surveillance, propaganda, etc. that taking any critical distance seems impossible. Just what would it mean to try to undertake a flaneur-like tour through the accumulated image culture of the 2020s? And could it be carried out in the same spirit in which Benjamin approached his *Arcades Project*?

Certainly, the idea of walking the glitzy streets of hyperspace with the intention of documenting it and thereby revealing its links to the history of capitalist domination would seem well-intentioned. There is, after all, a well-documented mass of young left-leaning meme producers, shitposters, YouTube video makers, and streamers who seem as yet unable or unready to manifest or get close to real political power (if we discount examples of Twitch streamers such as Hbomberguy or Lance from "The Serfs" appearing in Twitch streams with Alexandria Ocasio-Cortez). Perhaps, though, they could better understand power by taking a look around at the vast cultural depository they are embedded within — the internet.

Though before diving headlong into what would be a very long and involved project, it is worth asking if Benjamin's basic formulation as outlined here holds true today. Do the characteristics of online media, which are quite distinct from any prior media form, not distinguish it from the Benjaminian phantasmagoria? Most importantly: can the audience reconfigure history in new constellations given the proximity of power to the act of viewing in a data economy (if such a possibility ever existed)?

In considering this question, it is important to note that, as with many terms in Benjamin's output, the origins of the term phantasmagoria are not entirely defined. In one interpretation it represents a group of commodities that together have a spell-like effect on the viewer, similar to that of a phantasmagoric scene of the eighteenth century, wherein props and lighting would be used to create ghost-like effects. Yet in another, it simply describes the mechanism of commodity fetishism, the process by which the commodity exerts an influence on the human purchaser or owner based on assumed properties extraneous to it (for example, the toothpaste that makes you smile more). The distinction here is significant as, on the one hand, we have the possibility for assemblages of objects to create specific meanings, yet on the other, we have a blanket effect of commodification. The former allows for varied possibilities in terms of constellations of different objects producing different effects. The latter definition suggests an imposed homogeneity — i.e. the absolute commodification of society as people become slaves to objects. The key to understanding these two different versions of phantasmagoria with their wildly differing outcomes is another loosely defined term of Benjamin's, the "dialectical image."

The dialectical image is a notion that permeates *The Arcades Project*, and which was reportedly originally born from conversations between Benjamin and, variously, Adorno, Gretel

Adorno, Horkheimer, and Benjamin's long-term mistress, Asja Lacis. Aside from in *The Arcades Project*, it has no clear elucidation, meaning we are left with the notes that make up that opus to try and fathom what is meant by it. This has given many theorists a headache, as they try to piece together a method and potential praxis linked to the term.

In doing so, they often seize upon the idea of the dialectical image as a kind of shock, which comes about as an image-object delivers a bolt from the past that disrupts the present with a rude awakening — the recognition of our existence in the finite "present" moment. As Susan Buck-Morss, author of *Dialectics of Seeing: Walter Benjamin and The Arcades Project*, recounted, describing the design for the tomb of Robert Cecil (1536 to 1612) by Maximillian Colt, located in England:

> The finished sarcophagus combines a peaceful representation of James's advisor on the upper table with a carved skeleton beneath. The figuration unites two discourses — that of the life past, and the body's literal futurity — with an unseen but implied third term, that of the spirit. The spatial division of the entablature implies not only the proximity of the world of the living with the world of the dead but also, through its vertical axis, the distillation of the spirit from the body.[33]

This description, which Buck-Morss reportedly likened to Benjamin's dialectical image, draws a constellation between life and death (with Robert Cecil, 1st Earl of Sailsbury, depicted alive and as a skeleton), or past and present brought together momentarily via the artistic depiction itself. For those unfamiliar with the sculpture, which is only poorly documented on Google Images, the "Coffin Dance" meme serves as a garish contemporary equivalent, featuring a number of besuited Ghanian pallbearers dancing with a loaded coffin. This meme originally came to international prominence as a YouTube video of the phenomenon was uploaded in 2015 by user "Travelin Sister." At the time of writing, the video has over 6 million views, though the coffin dancers came to prominence as a viral meme when Facebook user Bigscout Nana Prempeth uploaded a video of a group of Ghanian dancing pallbearers dropping a coffin, in May 2019. Following this, the pallbearer video was appended to numerous "FAILS" (accidents and embarrassing situations) by users across TikTok, YouTube, Instagram, Facebook, and Tumblr. These videos often cut from scenes of a protagonist in some kind of life affirmative act, such as performing a bicycle wheelie or climbing a makeshift wall, to that of a coffin being carried by pallbearers. The viewer is then subjected to a "shock" as the coffin is accidentally dropped by the bearers, as they dance to a superimposed club anthem. This shock as life passes to death mirrors the "drop" of the marble Robert Cecil who can be seen in his monument depicted as flesh incarnate on the higher horizontal plane of his multi-tiered tomb, then as a skeleton on the lower level.

The moment of the dialectical image is the point at which we as viewers of the tomb or meme are snapped into ourselves as we feel the past intersect with the present finite moment, shocking us out of a complacent acceptance of our alienation at the hands of capital (though Cecil's tomb as a *memento mori* was presumably supposed to shock the viewer out of their complacent life of sin and distance from God). However, this is pretty much a description of Adorno's "shudder" which shocks the viewer out of accepting the false conditions of capitalism as he or she struggles to make sense of an abstract artwork or music score. Yet we can ascertain from letter exchanges that Benjamin and Adorno differ in their treatment of the artwork and what it does to disrupt capitalism. This difference is laid out in a letter of August 2, 1935 written by Adorno to Benjamin, to which Benjamin replied on December 27, 1935.[34]

The dispute revolves around a passage in Benjamin's

Arcades in which Benjamin states that "each era dreams of the next," a phrase Adorno seizes upon to express a deeper concern with Benjamin's method. Namely, it is overly dependent on the subjective process of dreaming, or the imagination, and as such overlooks the materialist impulse that Marx considered to be the motor of history. Adorno argues:

> If you transpose the dialectical image as a "dream" into consciousness, then not only has the concept been demystified and rendered sociable, but precisely through this it has forfeited the objective liberating power that could legitimize it materialistically.[35]

Put otherwise, Adorno wished to state that any truth content emerging from the artwork would have to be on account of its materiality and not of the imagination either of its producer or the audience. It is the imagination, rather, that arises from the material conditions of an artwork or commodity and the world it was produced in. It is those material conditions, embedded in the artwork, that for Adorno result in a moment of shock for the viewer of the radically abstract artwork as they are exposed to the reality of the human's link to the natural object and the impossibility of surpassing that link (and our mortality) via scientific discovery or capitalist production. This shock, or "shudder," is felt as a feeling of oneness with the artwork, and therefore the wider natural object, is interrupted by the realization that the work comprises components that arise from human labor, and thereby reveal our estrangement from nature through capitalism.

However, despite Adorno's objection, Benjamin's phrase remained in *The Arcades Project*, following on from a description of how industrial processes came to replace the building and artistic production of wish symbols (churches, religious icons, etc). The resulting industrially engineered buildings were then utilized for the further production or sale of industrial commodities. Though Benjamin argues, "they linger on the threshold" as something of the cultic past of objects — and the desire to escape that past — can be read into their present. Yet, at the same time, Benjamin continued, we can read the future based on our current dreams:

> Every epoch, in fact, not only dreams the one to follow but, in dreaming, precipitates its awakening. It bears its end within itself and unfolds it — as Hegel already noticed — by cunning. With the destabilizing of the market economy, we begin to recognize the monuments of the bourgeoisie as ruins even before they have.[36]

Commodities, buildings, artworks, allow us to teleologically trace our past and to forecast the future. This for Adorno appears fanciful, giving too much power to the subjective mind, which risks an upending of the hard-earned materialist turn of Marx. And yet, Benjamin clearly links the human imagination in any given epoch to its material output, and vice versa. Given this, Adorno's criticisms of Benjamin appear more as grapplings with the conscience of the bourgeois Institute for Social Research as an entity than specific criticisms of Benjamin's work (though they were that *too*). This would appear evident in a letter written by Adorno to Benjamin in November 1938, in which he alludes to long and worried conversations with Horkheimer over Benjamin's Arcades, stating that, put succinctly, there is too much given over to descriptions of flaneurism, arcades, and modernism, with not enough given over to the process of materialist mediation.[37] That is to say, the act of being a flaneur, or rather the experience of seeing Paris as a flaneur, is described more than the experience of the historical and material history that led to bourgeois flaneurism. We can find sympathy with Adorno if we consider that the section specifically on flaneurism, called simply "The Flaneur," contains reams and reams of esoteric quotes from Baudelaire, De Dumas, Dickens, Jung, alongside observations such as this:

In 1839 it was considered elegant to take a tortoise out walking. This gives us an idea of the tempo of flanerie in the arcades.[38]

Or this:

The attitude of the flaneur — epitome of the political attitude of the middle classes during the Second Empire.[39]

And one might agree with Adorno that quotes like these lack a sense of urgency as regards preparedness for Marxist-Leninist revolution (or anything approaching it) — except, of course, Adorno looked barely prepared himself. In any case, in a society where industrial building processes are key to the economy, who has time to take a tortoise for a walk? Only surely a beneficiary of capitalism. Indeed, tortoise walking (apparently a popular pastime in early-nineteenth century Paris) brings to mind some of the more frivolous meme formats, demonstrating the absolute dearth of purpose or meaning in the lives of young people living in developed nations. These include the practice of lip-synching to lines from movies or dancing to 15-second segments of songs (15 seconds being the maximum length of a TikTok video, although four videos can be strung together into a one-minute sequence). Specific dance routines include *The WAP*, based on thrusting moves from the video to Cardi B and Megan Thee Stallion's hit song, and *Tap In*, set to SAweetie's homonymous song. These moves are emulated by tens to hundreds of thousands of mostly female amateur dancers who can command as many as millions of views each. While incomparable to taking tortoises for a walk, in their utter uselessness and studied, even forced, casualness they share something in common with the flaneur. And here it is worth bearing in mind that only a perverse material reality could have made going for a walk with a tortoise "in 1839" seem like a good idea. These material realities are also what made, again, "The attitude of the flaneur," the "epitome of the political attitude of the middle classes during the Second Empire." This attitude, which is far from one of action, is arguably the same one that makes young women, and sometimes men, contort themselves today to fit the oblong frame of the smartphone (the dimensions of a TikTok video), the dimensions of which make their sexualized movements appear hideously automated.

Anyone who has seen young people preparing a dance for social media will note the amount of time they put into rehearsing and re-enacting the dance, erasing the prior recording until they get it just right. As Mark Fisher observed in relation to SMS text messages during a talk given at the University of Warwick in 2011:

...it's typical for teenagers to spend, you know, up to an hour comprising an sms text message of 150 characters just to assure they get the right level of nonchalance.[40]

What this tells us is that while what often appears relaxed is actually labor, this is only ultimately achievable due to there being a lack of a requirement to labor in the workplace, or at school. This is indeed the proverbial elephant in the room — that which cannot be said but which is more than apparent — that Benjamin reveals with both his fixation on flaneurism and the way he assembles factoids and quotes about bourgeois Paris without peppering them with calls to arms. That elephant in the room regards the level to which the cozy existence the bourgeois class enjoyed in Paris in the nineteenth century was equaled by Benjamin's and Adorno's existence, which while blighted by the horrors of World War Two, was relatively insulated compared to their working-class Jewish counterparts or to political dissidents in Germany.

The point is, the flaneur walks and observes idly as that is the assigned role of much of the bourgeois class. As Benjamin says in "The Flaneur" chapter of *The Arcades Project*: "the idleness of the flaneur is a demonstration against the division of labor."[41] Being — as is often the case in *The Arcades Project* — that this sentence is sandwiched between two others that bear little relation to it, it is difficult to suppose exactly what form Benjamin saw this protest as taking. Though he likely meant that the stilted slow movements of the flaneur, taking in the Paris Arcades and their resplendent commodities as well as decor, formed a refusal to partake in industrial society, as much as a rhetorical pose and question, "What else do you expect me to do?" The French bourgeois class, stuck between a past where their aristocratic overbears were guillotined and a future in which they themselves were to be deposed, might well see little else to do but observe in awe the detritus of history congealed in capitalist objects. Those who are more disposed to speed up the process of the ascension of the working class to power might try to configure in their minds that detritus, those commodities, drawing constellations between them that might act as a call for arms. They might observe the frivolousness in the juxtaposition between glamour models on magazine covers, headlines of war on newspaper front pages, patterned floral designs on bars of soap, intricate bejeweled rings that mimic the cast-iron arbors of nineteenth-century industrial warehouses. They may then deduce from this the perversity of class relations that led to our society today, out of the imaginations of men who enslaved others, saying "let it be thus," simply because they crave power. This is the purpose of both Benjamin's fascination with the flaneur and his innate personal flaneurism. It is distinct from the shock that characterizes Adorno's shudder. Indeed,

Benjamin wrote cryptically in another fragmentary sentence in *The Arcades Project* that:

> In my formulation: The eternal is in any case far more the ruffle on a dress than some idea. Dialectical Image.[42]

For Benjamin, the heroic, the shock, the calamitous were not necessary marks of an awareness of the true conditions of capital, perhaps as he saw these conditions all around him and felt the bourgeois complicity with capitalism so much that he wished to enunciate it in all its banality.

This is not for a moment to equate bourgeois experience with working-class experience, in terms of awareness of the reality of class struggle. Yet, the ability for relatively privileged people to grasp the reality of class struggle remains as fundamental today as it always has been. This is because, however much the working class and lower-middle class of Western countries struggle, they are hugely more privileged than the productive classes of Asia, Africa, and South America. At the same time, it is worth considering the extent to which we today enjoy conveniences that were unimaginable to the affluent bourgeois scholars of the Frankfurt School. As such, parallels can be seen with Benjamin's practice as a hash-addled flaneur taking in the sites of the Paris streets and arcades and today's digital flaneur, who dedicates portions of her or his day to observing other people, their memes, and online stores: or with friendship duos who spend hours contorting themselves to fit the rectangular proportions of their phone screen in a manner that looks more-or-less effortless. All so they can share the resulting 15-second long TikTok video to gain the adoration of other friends, who have been doing the same thing all day.

The task for the online left is to develop for the mass of relatively privileged Western "digital flaneurs" a practice of observing the phantasmagoria comprised of digital objects, from video games to social media platforms, to memes, YouTube, insta, and TikTok videos, WhatsApp, and telegram chats, Amazon storefront, Netflix, Hulu, Twitch, and so on. From there it remains to piece together the fragmented visual representations of reality and to make from the momentary glimpse of the past and future intersecting in the dialectical image a new constellation of objects that allows for reformulated economic reality. It could not be made clearer that this would represent the best Benjaminian practice for today's leftist meme kid than in Benjamin's letter to his friend and spiritual confidante Gerhard Sholem written on October 24, 1935. At the letter's end, Benjamin confided that the series of reflections he had given form under the title *The Work of Art in the Age of Mechanical Reproduction*, "anchor the history of nineteenth-century art in the recognition of their situation as experienced by us in the present."[43]

That is to say, Benjamin has intended to apprehend via *The Work of Art in the Age of Mechanical Reproduction*, the material fact and sequence of events that led to the (then) current historical moment via a consideration of its specific media composition: TV, radio, mass publications. What he saw, as discussed here in Chapter 2, was the accumulation of uneven property relations coming to expression via the grievances of mass media audiences who felt cheated given the gap between what the media offered and what was actually available to them. Today, we take aloof flaneur-like walks through digital arcades replete with memes and videos co-opted as data commodities. In doing so, we might take time to assemble constellations of these image objects so as to reconstruct from them the history of capitalism and to allow possible future assemblages conducive to a socialist vision. This may require a slowing down of our media consumption, not to a turtle's pace, but enough to make reflection upon the mechanisms underlying our current digital era of capitalism possible. In this way, as we look back on the accumulated debris of history, like Klee's angel of history, we will be able to reconfigure it rather than be configured by it. This is how "each era may dream of the next," and it comes about as a seizing of the truth of the material relations of the present through the apprehension of cultural or architectural objects (the moment of the dialectical image). The Dancing Coffin as a dialectical image may lead us to realize our mortality and the fact that we are alive now, and therefore need to make use of our short lifespans. Yet if you are truly a digital flaneur you'd stop to reflect on the masses of Western teens and adults who routinely laugh at the funereal rights of the people of Ghana (an ex-Portuguese, then British colony) and the workers who dance as they carry coffins. Before then reflecting on the Western zoomers and millennials that contort themselves to achieve the right "look" for videos that serve to enrich the data economy, asking yourself, "How did history arrive here?"

Chapter 6

Psychedelic Dreams: Marcuse, Fisher, and Acid Communism

If Benjamin comes across at points as a hapless dreamer and Adorno and Horkheimer as agitated and curmudgeonly elitists, Marcuse is a kind of estranged slightly cooler relative to his aloof colleagues of the Frankfurt School. While both Adorno and Horkheimer returned to Germany post World War Two to help rebuild Germany, Marcuse stayed in the US. For Adorno and Horkheimer their move eventually meant coming up against students who wanted — as part of the wave of protests that swept Europe in the late 1960s — to upend industrial bourgeois society, who they sternly warned of the dangers of hoping for too much. Marcuse, in contrast, became deeply involved in the US student protests, becoming a kind of awkward but much-loved granddaddy to the 1960s movement, rubbing shoulders and exchanging strategies with none other than activist and philosopher Angela Davis.

It's hard to say who this reflects worse on in hindsight: Adorno for refusing to join his students in fermenting a societal uprising from campus, or Marcuse, as the very unlikely face of a new social and sexual permissiveness in America. Today we tend to perceive that the gender and civil rights movements should be led by representatives of the groups that seek empowerment. Black Lives Matter urge that white protestors yield to the authority of any present black comrades in any given situation. In this light, it's hard to see what Marcuse had to offer the African-American Angela Davis. But when you consider that Adorno tried to deter Davis from returning from Frankfurt (where she studied at Frankfurt University) to the US to join the protest movement altogether, Marcuse immediately emerges as the more progressive of the two. As Davis has stated, Adorno "suggested that my desire to work directly in the radical movements of that period was akin to a media studies scholar deciding to become a radio technician."[44]

In any case, it is safe to say that the absolute prominence in twentieth-century aesthetic theory of a few bourgeois German men (to which we can add some Frenchmen, such as Debord, Lyotard, and Baudrillard) is very much a symptom of history and the extent to which higher academic study was restricted to wealthy white men until very recently. It is perhaps the bourgeois background of Adorno, Benjamin, Horkheimer, and Marcuse that prevented them from proposing some kind of incendiary direction for the left (indeed, they in some cases impeded it). Ultimately, their work is collectively concerned with the consideration of entirely harmless subject areas. Sure, they turned the focus of academia to popular culture and identified class subjugation at play in the offerings of the culture industry, yet aren't endless reflections on media objects liable to detract precisely from any action that might be taken to overthrow the system itself? And here you see, perhaps, Adorno's real interest (and lack of understanding) in comparing activism to becoming a radio technician. For Adorno, both activism and manual labor in the service of the culture industry amounted to tinkering at the service of a vast societal mechanism that would ultimately anyhow be subject to the antagonisms of class and race division. This was assured by a basically flawed mode of human thinking that leads us to "identify" and categorize nature and humans in a bid to control them. All that a protest might achieve, if anything, was to rejig the social spectrum so that one set of humans would have control of the mass, instead of another, as evidenced in the rise of European Fascism and Soviet Communism. But isn't this the kind of judgment that only a comfortably middle-class person can make (even acknowledging the horror of being a German Jew who fled the Nazis)?

For Davis, as for a great many other people, the gamble one takes on a protest march is that any resultant improvement will be a worthwhile investment for yourself and your family and friends, as well as others like yourself. And any possible worsening in life conditions as a result of protest is worth the gamble, given how bad things are for your family, friends, and others like you. What is interesting here, though, is that the same could be said for a technician's job at a radio station! And what many readers may be thinking is that they'd quite like either to be involved in a radical protest movement that would be taken as seriously in reflection — still decades later — as the Black Panthers or to be a radio technician (or successful podcast producer). Ultimately, they'd probably be happy to do both. Here we can see that the stakes for the main protagonists of the Frankfurt School were very different than for many people, which is perhaps precisely why the content of their books amounts largely to reflection on aesthetic and abstract philosophical phenomena — i.e. because hazarding a revolution wasn't at any point a better option than writing polemic critiques about TV, film, and radio. They had nothing to gain in doing so, given their relative affluence and the opportunity it gave them to sit things out in university departments rather than getting their hands dirty with street protest (or radio technician work). As suggested, Marcuse here was the exception, in that he became a regular attendant and speaker at protests in the US. Though here he is accused of being a chief progenitor of the New Left, a loose movement of thinkers, politicians, and bureaucrats from Noam Chomsky to Susan Sontag to Gore Vidal, who shifted the focus of the left from the workplace and its relations to the body, race, and sexuality. Again, such a move, from a man whose family owned a textile factory, may have its own class-based rationale in the sense that the New Left ended up blunting the canine teeth of the left by limiting it to the soft targets of race, gender, and sexual equality or freedom, without addressing material inequality. Now this would all be intensely damning for the Frankfurt School, which probably had no intention of permanently blighting the left. That is, unless there could be seen to be something of strategic use today in the texts they have left to us. Though before we get on to that, it is worth considering Marcuse's wider philosophical position. Marcuse effectively libidinized Adorno and Horkheimer's bitter and po-faced critique of the culture industry made in the *Dialectic of Enlightenment*, itself based on Marx's materialist critique of societal conditions. The application of Marx to the sphere of culture by Adorno and Horkheimer brought alienation into the realm of matters of taste, which could no longer be enjoyed with leisurely reflection, given culture's co-optation to capitalism. The trouble was, this left little room for the reentry of human emotions, aesthetic preferences, or desires, stripping the left of any recourse to an autonomous culture with which to critique the status quo. For the post-war left, the revolution would have to be as mechanistic as capitalism was and as human life had become. Even Adorno's shudder occurring in the face of the abstract artwork recalling primordial fear in face of nature and thereby momentarily shaking the human individual from their induced stupor seems terribly procedural and peculiarly lacking in the possibility of enjoyment.

One can understand this with Adorno, given both the dire state of the world at the end of World War Two and his naturally melancholic predisposition. Anything so frivolous as enjoyment was likely anyhow a second-rate form of entertainment aimed at keeping people docile. As Adorno and Horkheimer wrote in *Dialectic of Enlightenment*, in an advanced capitalist society, "There is laughter because there is nothing to laugh about." Laughter signals acceptance of the thorough commodification of society engaged in as a kind of feigned ignorance at our complicity with the culture industry. Laughter is, the Frankfurt duo continues, "the instrument for cheating happiness. To moments of happiness laughter is foreign; only operettas, and now films, present sex amid peals of merriment."[45]

As it happens, Marcuse also felt that enjoyment had been thwarted, though precisely as it had been permitted to the masses openly and in line with modified desires, so as to satiate them and keep them dependent on the capitalist machine. In this way, capitalism performed the feat of satisfying what Freud called the "pleasure principle" without threatening the social order. Indeed, the restrictive aesthetic and industrial reality of late capitalist society for Marcuse limits the bounds of the human imagination, negating the ability for desire to be turned outward as a creative appropriation of libido.

As Marcuse explains in a passage that reads like watching a filmic sex scene as a teen with your parents in the room:

>...compare love-making in a meadow and in an automobile, on a lovers' walk outside the town walls and on a Manhattan street. In the former cases, the environment partakes of and invites libidinal cathexis and tends to be eroticized. Libido transcends beyond the immediate erotogenic zones — a process of non-repressive sublimation. In contrast, a mechanized environment seems to block such self-transcendence of libido. Impelled in the striving to extend the field of erotic gratification, libido becomes less "polymorphous," less capable of eroticism beyond localized sexuality, and the latter is intensified. Thus diminishing erotic and intensifying sexual energy, the technological reality limits the scope of sublimation.[46]

In short, the process of "sublimation," which in Freudian terms safely dispenses with desires that might otherwise challenge the status quo, is so far dulled that the scope of human endeavor is greatly hampered (via a process of "repressive desublimation"). Industrial capitalist society, while offering apparent free choices, plays the trick of both satiating desire and limiting desire's creative potential. As Marcuse argues:

> The environment from which the individual could obtain pleasure — which he could cathect as gratifying almost as an extended zone of the body — has been rigidly reduced. Consequently, the "universe" of libidinous cathexis is likewise reduced. The effect is a localization and contraction of libido, the reduction of erotic to sexual experience and satisfaction.[47]

These reflections have stood the test of time well, having been presented in *One Dimensional Man* in 1964. At the time the book propelled Marcuse to fame in the US, given the trend toward sexual openness and the challenging of the restrictive processes deriving from "tradition" and the exigencies of the capitalist system of production and consumption. What Marcuse pointed to was the existence under capitalism of a promiscuity encouraged in order to maintain, not challenge, the power structure. Such promiscuity would benefit the system as raw sexual function surpassed amorousness, thereby dulling the creative and risqué elements that accompany or derive from sex and sexual urges. This was not to say that promiscuity should be discouraged, far from it. Though this was simply the wrong sort, resulting in sex that maintained the status quo. Which is about as unsexy a concept as one can imagine.

Fast forward to the 2020s and this is still a paramount concern, and to a degree that Marcuse possibly couldn't have foreseen. What passed for permissiveness in the 1960s would appear staid by today's standards, as graphic porn is readily available on ubiquitous devices, and mainstream TV and film feature a level of sexualization perpetually verging at least on salaciousness. Eroticism has itself assumed a memetic quality as amateur models frequently become "insta famous" by posting near-nude selfie images, or make money on platforms such as OnlyFans, which allows models to charge a subscription for nude or semi-nude photos of themselves. These platforms of course bring in a level of choice and, potentially, an empowerment that is difficult to dismiss as somehow "controlled." Perhaps here it makes sense to dispense with the relative notion of "freedom of choice" and to simply ask to what extent people are subjugated today, irrespective of the choices they make. Such an approach not only cuts right through the problem of people thinking they are free while being actually subjugated (as Marcuse argues they were in the 1960s), but is also particularly apt in the social media era, where constant choice is the motor of entertainment (rather than, say, choosing a film and then sitting still for 90 minutes).

Here both the experience of the creator and user of pornographic material might be instructive (and many readers will anyhow be either one, the other, or both), in that generally neither party finds the situation of making or using porn to be an ideal expression of their sexual and romantic desire. If they do, then Marcuse's thesis that capitalism only satiates desire as it limits what the capitalist subject *actually desires* is almost certainly true. As he argued early on in *One Dimensional Man*:

> If the worker and his boss enjoy the same television program and visit the same resort places, if the typist is as attractively made up as the daughter of her employer, if the Negro owns a Cadillac, if they all read the same newspaper, then this assimilation indicates not the disappearance of classes, but the extent to which the needs and satisfactions that serve the preservation of the Establishment are shared by the underlying population.[48]

That is to say, if we all enjoy a certain level of comfort, it does not mean that we are all comfortable, but rather that capitalism has adjusted our base level of acceptable comfort. The same could be said, more or less, with regard to desire — in that any degree of satiation accords with a redefinition of desire itself. This is in part because desire is effectively something we can only feel toward things we don't have. Though beyond this, even momentary satiation of sexual desire is today often achieved at the fulfillment of something so banal and easily achieved (the opening of a web page) that the sexual functioning is reduced to being just another human need that can be satisfied by a phone browser.

Of course, there is a debate over whether or not a woman's, or man's, ability to earn money from posting images of herself online might constitute empowerment, yet it would be a very specific desire that held as its principal aim the production of nude selfies for sale online. That is to say, there may be some degree of satisfaction in providing sexualized images to paying subscribers, but this doesn't mean the provider *is not subjugated.* One only needs to recall the 19-year-old Belle Delphine selling her "used bathwater" as "Gamer Girl Bathwater" to fans on her Patreon account for $30 for a small bottle. After all, it is possible to conceive of a society in which Delphine wouldn't want or need to sell her used bathwater in order to feel economically or sexually fulfilled. As Marcuse argued in 1964:

> This society turns everything it touches into a potential source of progress and of exploitation, of drudgery and satisfaction, of freedom and of oppression. Sexuality is no exception.[49]

From the purview of the male user of online sexual services and material (the market for Delphine's bathwater), the meme "Are You Winning, Son?" speaks of the awkwardness of a culture that is both permissive and repressed. The meme, which derives from a comic panel probably first published in 2014 on 4Chan, features a crude MS Paint drawing of a father arriving home and asking "Are ya winning, Son?" to his gamer offspring. In the original comic the son has a VR headset on and is saying "please please play with my breasts" to a character that he is interacting with, in the virtual realm.[50] The meme resurfaced in 2020 in many variants, though what is most interesting here is the way in which the father in the meme inadvertently yet accurately describes the status of sex as an activity that can be "won" in the twenty-first century. Belle Delphine, who released a real sex video to her OnlyFans audience on Christmas Day 2020, would be an ostensible winner of the sex "game," given the vast amounts of money she makes from male fans. However, her eventual making of a real porn video 18 months after teasing fans with deceptively titled videos uploaded to PornHub shows that she may not be entirely in control of her own image. While those earlier videos featured titles such as *Belle Delphine Strokes Two BIG Cocks*, leading to a video of Delphine stroking two live roosters, her Christmas Day porn video featured hardcore sex acts. For many, this signaled a fall from grace, not specifically because she performed real sex acts on camera, but because she lost her critical edge in doing so. After all, Delphine had previously been famed for hubristically offering everything to her fans and delivering nothing.

Of course, she still has an adoring army of male fans, yet capitalism ultimately ruined her pretense to autonomy from the system by leading her to engage in the banalest possible act she herself could have engaged in for the public: actual sex. Ultimately, Marcuse's assertion that capitalism dulls sexual desire holds true today as the mechanical act of performed sex deadens the titillation that pushes desire in all directions, spurring creativity as a form of sublimation that delivers creative and political action as a side effect of unfulfillment (whereas capitalism leads people to mistake the unfulfilling solo-cyber-sex with fulfillment itself). Though the possibility of regaining creative sublimation is indicated by Delphine's earlier acts, which performed a critique of the emptiness of desire in the twenty-first century.

Ultimately, like Adorno and Horkheimer, and indeed Fisher, Marcuse felt that there may be some glimmer of hope to be caught within an otherwise bleak social structure. For Marcuse, this hope resided in the possibility of redirecting the powers of sublimation by harnessing the creativity of the student and hippy movements of the 1960s, as well as: "the substratum of the outcasts and outsiders, the exploited and persecuted of other races and other colors, the unemployed and unemployable."[51] These groups, which Marcuse saw as existing "beneath the conservative popular base," live, he argued, in conditions of such urgency and need that they are by nature revolutionary in their evasion of technocratic society's tendency to fulfill basic human desires (however much those desires are modified by capitalism in the first place). As Marcuse continues:

Thus their opposition is revolutionary even if their consciousness is not. Their opposition hits the system from without and is therefore not deflected by the system; it is an elementary force which violates the rules of the game and, in doing so, reveals it as a rigged game. When they get together and go out into the streets, without arms, without protection, in order to ask for the most primitive civil rights, they know that they face dogs, stones, and bombs, jail, concentration camps, even death. Their force is behind every political demonstration for the victims of law and order. The fact that they start refusing to play the game may be the fact which marks the beginning of the end of a period.[52]

These thoughts constitute the conclusion to *One Dimensional Man* via, in the preceding chapter, a call to art to ameliorate the aspect of technology that ultimately deadens rather than satisfies human desire. Though, like Adorno, Marcuse sees the potential of art, which is a more honest reflection of the human psyche than technology, as ultimately blighted by technocratic society:

> In various forms of mask and silence, the artistic universe is organized by the images of a life without fear — in mask and silence because art is without power to bring about this life, and even without power to represent it adequately.[53]

This tragic hampering of art's potential in envisioning new and utopian realities evokes "The World if..." (otherwise known as "How Society Would Look," or "Imagine the World Without") meme. The World if meme features a utopian eco-city environment beneath a caption such as: "society if vegans were in charge"; "society if dads went to therapy"; or — a meta critique worthy of postmodern philosophers — "the world if everybody would stop posting memes." Often these memes are meant in irony as an exaggeration of, or outright joke upon, the importance of a given activity. One can imagine various forms of the meme addressing, for example, the value of art to society. For one, we could make a version that reads "the world if contemporary art didn't exist," suggesting that the commodification of art as a luxury investor product has been the death knell for any hope of using art's redemptive qualities to counter capitalism. We might, conversely, imagine a version depicting a dystopia (as is often seen in one variant of the meme) reading "society if art did not exist," signaling the redemptive qualities of art that is not co-opted by capital.

For Marcuse society would ultimately flourish if the ostensibly rational aspects of technology could be dialectically melded with the capacity for art to dream up and make visible the unthinkable. Though with art being ultimately secondary to a kind of false rationality that reduces human ambition through an offering of tepid alternatives to our unfettered fantasy, Marcuse envisions its role as one of protest in favor of a society where it could play a wider role in the exploration and amelioration of human desire:

> Whether ritualized or not, art contains the rationality of negation. In its advanced positions, it is the Great Refusal — the protest against that which is. The modes in which man and things are made to appear, to sing and sound and speak, are modes of refuting, breaking, and recreating their factual existence.[54]

This is where Marcuse and Adorno strongly differ, both on the page and in the real world, where their respective stances led them to intense disagreement in the late 1960s. This disagreement came about in short for Adorno's caution regarding the probability — as he saw it — that any strongly revolutionary or reactionary movement would repeat the problems of past and ongoing revolutions. As Adorno wrote to Marcuse in the last letter to be written in a correspondence that took place in 1969 between philosophers of, by then, international standing:

> I am the last person to underestimate the merits of the student movement; it has disrupted the smooth transition to the totally administered world. But it contains a grain of insanity in which a future totalitarianism is implicit.[55]

With regard to this quote, and given Adorno's reputation as a curmudgeonly bourgeois intellectual, it is important to realize that firstly, the stated "grain of insanity" must not be taken as a conservative shying from the nature of protest itself. The grain of insanity which Adorno identifies is the tendency toward domination that characterizes rationalist thought, which seeks to dominate unfettered nature, but results in a domination of man by man, and then of "capital" over all men. Until this grain of madness is shifted there will be no move away from systems of domination, and any movement which attempts this will be caught up in the antagonisms of power struggle only to be defeated, or to become dominant themselves, and in such a way that perpetuates domination.

The correspondence from which the quote originates centered around Marcuse wishing to side with Adorno's students who had occupied the faculty of Frankfurt University where Adorno held his professorship. At one point Marcuse upset Adorno by asking that he could address the students personally upon his return to Germany during the 1969 summer break, as he often did in the US, believing those students to be part of the Great Refusal of technocracy that he encouraged, rather than a breakaway horde that threatened philosophy's autonomy from politics (which Adorno cherished), and thereby its ability to critique capitalism:

> But I do believe that there are situations, moments, in which theory is pushed on further by praxis — situations and moments in which theory that is kept separate from praxis becomes untrue to itself.[56]

Adorno responded that the risk resided in the student movement turning into its opposite as a result of its loss of critical distance from society, and further added that Marcuse's criticism of the Vietnam war, a central rallying call of the student movement worldwide (particularly in the US where Marcuse had become an unlikely icon of the protest movement) had an ideological element so long as he would not condemn torture at the hands of the Viet Cong. This element is key, for it signals the extent to which Adorno would not be drawn in support of any system or ideology, as much as he despised rampant US capitalism.

Marcuse's counter-response drives to the heart of the

problem faced by academia during moments of mass uprising:

> Like you, I believe it is irresponsible to sit at one's writing
> desk advocating activities to people who are fully prepared
> to let their heads be bashed in for the cause.[57]

What is then suggested is that a new theory, equal to the moment
of political praxis, is needed, so that whatever philosophy has
to tell to young protestors might be of use on the streets, and
then in the debating chambers when it comes to implementing
policy. The key to the debate resides in whether all opposing
political and social forces go toward making up a whole within
which they are consigned to re-enact the forces of domination,
or whether some forces may be able to transcend domination
by standing outside that rotten social whole. For both thinkers,
the latter was the hope, but for Adorno any such hope of
transcendence will always be liable to revert back into the
negative social whole which it inevitably anyhow derives from.

Echoing and expanding upon the opening quote here, Adorno
finishes his correspondence with Marcuse on the subject of the
student uprising in the following way, giving the lie to those
who perceive him as having been ensconced within the safety
that his mere theorizing supposedly enabled. Following on
directly from the above quote regarding the dram of madness
inherent in the student of movement, he continues:

> And I am not a masochist, not when it comes to theory.
> Furthermore, the German situation really is different. By the
> way, in an exam recently, I got another dose of tear gas; that
> is most burdensome, given my severe conjunctivitis.[58]

While this goes some way to dismissing the notion that Adorno
was led by a bourgeois fear of violence, in that he apparently
suffered some minor effects of tear-gassing, as well as being

threatened and harassed by his students, it also flatly contradicts his main premise. Ultimately, despite Adorno's desire to keep theory separate from praxis, he still suffered the slings and arrows of conflict. Indeed, he was famously humiliated by students when he tried to begin lectures earlier in that summer's semester as he was disrupted by students writing "If Adorno is left in peace, capitalism will never cease" on the blackboard, before three female students exposed their bare breasts, while stood at the front of the lecture hall. The *Busenattentat* (or 'breast action') took place on April 22, 1969, although it was part of a sustained campaign involving a student occupation led by Adorno's PhD student Hans-Jürgen Krahl, which Adorno had earlier called the police to in January 1969.

Two weeks after the event Adorno gave an interview in the German newspaper *Der Spiegel*, where he expressed a kind of surprised disdain for the action, given his own opposition to "erotic repression and against sex taboos." Incredulously he stated:

To mock me and to incite three girls dressed up as hippies on me! I found that disgusting. The effect of amusement that you achieve with it was basically the reaction of the philistine, who goes "teehee!" and giggles when he sees a girl with bare breasts.[59]

Wittingly or not the students had unleashed upon Adorno a caricature of the permissive hippy movement that Marcuse had aligned himself with in the United States. In doing so, they arguably signaled the impotence of Marcuse's position as much as Adorno's. For if Marcuse's central argument was that society expended human desire in mechanistic acts of entertainment that ultimately fell short of delivering upon desire's full promise, was this erotically charged protest not indicative of even the protest movement's general failure to deliver more than spectacle? The Vietnam war ended in 1975, yet capitalism and the military-industrial complex have remained. Far from delivering us from technocracy, the accumulated anti-capitalist movements of the post-war period have coincided with a growth in the gap between rich and poor in the Western world and a level of technocratic monitoring and surveillance unimaginable in the late 1960s.

However, the promise of art remains present yet frustratingly elusive. Now, we can all be involved in creative production and dissemination, via the internet. Why shouldn't we see this as an opportunity to counter the considerable forces of technocracy, held up in part via the internet and to dialectically oppose them with creative productions — memes, video essays, etc. — aimed at upsetting the status quo?

In his essay *Aesthetic Dimension*, published in 1977, Marcuse provided a follow-up to *One Dimensional Man* and, in particular, allusions he made toward the latter's end about the capacity of artistic endeavor to overcome the controlling auspices of capitalism. At the time of publication, the Vietnam war had ended yet capitalism moved on unhindered. It was the eve of the birth of Thatcher's and Reagan's neoconservatism, which would morph over time into neoliberalism. The latter system, which is still dominant today despite Trumpism denting its superficial multicultural surface, has in part been so dominant precisely because it co-opted Marcuse's and the New Left's general call for a world of inclusion. The ethnic and economic underclasses that Marcuse saw as having so much potential due to their exclusion from the satiation of mostly neutered desires have either been assimilated within capitalism, or are so far outside the system as to make their incorporation in rebellion impossible. Even so, the words Marcuse writes about art remain true:

Inasmuch as art preserves, with the promise of happiness, the memory of the goal that failed, it can enter, as a "regulative idea," the desperate struggle for changing the world. Against all fetishism of the productive forces, against the continued enslavement of individuals by the objective conditions (which remain those of domination), art represents the ultimate goal of all revolutions: the freedom and happiness of the individual.[60]

Indeed such platitudes to art will likely always remain true, perhaps becoming more poignant the further from utopia we become. This is because art — synonymous with imagination — becomes fantastical in inverse proportion to reality, explaining why our dreams in covid lockdown have become especially vivid. It may also be why both the main figures of the Frankfurt School and Fisher found themselves curiously restricted to making vague allusions to the power of art as their only remedy to the autocratic barbarity of capitalism. As capitalism aims to reduce both the stimulus we encounter and our desire for it, such that our desires can be easily exhausted, it is our duty and biological imperative to fight back with more elaborate desires — be they political, erotic, or plain fantastical.

To this end, we might call upon the term "Acid Communism," coined by Mark Fisher in an unfinished book of the same name to denote a much-needed new counterculture equal to the hippy, punk, and rave movements of the 1960s to 1990s.[61] This idea has recently taken off in the meme sphere with a number of dedicated social media pages championing the Acid Communist and "Acid Corbynist" cause, yet its true potential arguably remains to be seen. While articles, seminars, lefttube videos, and meme images point to what Acid Communism might mean, there has not yet been a sustained real-world movement of happenings, concerts, seminars, and educational events. While the campaign group Momentum held Acid Corbynist events alongside the Labour Party Conference for consecutive years in 2017 and 2018, the term itself was heard little during the election campaign of 2019. After all, the terms "acid" and "communism" were hardly liable to have swung the election for Labour. Now that we are no longer in an election campaign, free from the obligations and burdens of power, both the UK and the US left have time to build a grassroots left movement that might achieve for the cultural landscape what the alt-right and QAnon did for white supremacy. The question is: what would constitute a non-violent "Acid Left" Capitol uprising? And why should the right-wing have the most bizarre protests and memes (with the anti-lockdown movement coalescing around David Icke in the UK in 2020 being a memorable example)? The ultimate aim of the online left, following Adorno's predilection to abstraction, Benjamin for the phantasmagoria, Marcuse for the Great Refusal, and Fisher for the harnessing of mental illness for revolutionary aims, should be to foster the conditions for "in real life" activity aimed at reclaiming our desire and creatively sublimating it to the fostering of a communitarian society. To get hung up on the policy details — whether anarchist, communist, or socialist — would be over cumbersome here, and indeed endless poring over the minutiae of left theory is directly counterproductive to the irrationalist aim of an Acid Left movement. What the online left should be doing in the wake of covid is encouraging far-out creative output that challenges the tendency of the data economy to push us toward quantitative goals both online and in real life.

Ultimately, art needs to be opposed to the drudgery of life under capitalism, with the former's promise of freedom being writ large all over our global banks and national stock exchanges. We need a Marcusian Great Refusal for our times. As Fisher explains in his introduction to "Acid Communism," published in the compendium *K-Punk: The Collected and Unpublished Writings of Mark Fisher (2004-2016)*:

The Great Refusal rejected, not only capitalist realism, but "realism" as such. There is, he wrote, an "inherent conflict between art and political realism." Art was a positive alienation, a "rational negation" of the existing order of things. His Frankfurt School predecessor, Theodor Adorno, had placed a similar value on the intrinsic alterity of experimental art. In Adorno's work, however, we are invited to endlessly examine the wounds of a damaged life under capital; the idea of a world beyond capital is dispatched into a utopian beyond. Art only marks our distance from this utopia. By contrast, Marcuse vividly evokes, as an immediate prospect, a world totally transformed. It was no doubt this quality of his work that meant Marcuse was taken up so enthusiastically by elements of the Sixties counterculture. He had anticipated the counterculture's challenge to a world dominated by meaningless labor.[62]

This approach will seem to some to be overblown, outlandish even. Yet ever since the start of modernism — when Kant attempted to account for the existence of a common ethics in the dumbfounded and irrational experience of witnessing beauty — it has been apparent that the communitarian cause transcends the logical faculties. Kant located the *sensus communis* (the "common sense") in the moment that our faculties of judgment evade us when confronted by unfathomable nature (a mountainscape for example). In so doing, he presaged the turbulence of modernism as humanity attempted to equal natural beauty (which we can all find agreement upon) by forcing an ethical system worthy of it. In the end, we managed only to mimic nature's propensity to chaos. In recent years, the right-wing has now openly adopted the irrationality that runs through nature as a smokescreen to hide their profit motive. It is up to the left to adopt irrationality as a motor for the irrational act of compassion — the one political calling that can justify our empty human existence.

It is from the depths of anxiety and depression that such an unrealistic mission arises. It is from the depths of psychosis that this calling is given an aesthetic form. These sicknesses — caused, as Fisher argues, by capitalism — carry a kaleidoscopic reordering function that colors human ethics in the rich, hypersensitive palette of a manic episode or psychedelic experience.

Of course, such experiences need mediating with objective experience. To achieve this, we need an incendiary subcultural movement that rips up the political and cultural canons that led us to the impasse we're at, realigning our vision via a reconfiguration of the constellations of image objects we find online. Like digital flaneurs we need to seamlessly incorporate our psychic reality with the image culture of online arcades at our own pace, seizing what's useful to challenge consumerist psychopathy and algorithm-pleasing cultural output along the way. Then we need to turn what we find outward onto the streets in the formation of a grassroots movement that can reconfigure the debris of capitalism in new community-based formations. This is the task of Acid Leftism in these coming years.

Endnotes

1   McManus, Matt and Watson, Mike. 2020. "This Is How Bernie Wins." *Merion West.* https://merionwest.com/2020/02/11/the-left-in-an-election-year/

2   Benjamin, Walter, p19. In: *Illuminations,* edited by Hannah Arendt, translated by Harry Zohn, from the 1935 essay. Schocken Books, 1969.

3   Benjamin, Walter, p12. As above.

4   For latest stats, see: https://twitchtracker.com/statistics

5   See: https://m.twitch.tv/joshuacitarella/clip/PlacidEasyGoshawkGivePLZ

6   Documentation can be seen here: https://www.youtube.com/watch?v=MVq8n1iMkO8

7   Attali, Jacques, p9. "Noise: The Political Economy of Music." Manchester University Press, 1985.

8   Attali, Jacques, p135. As above.

9   Sontag, Susan, pp1-27. *On Photography.* Penguin, 2002.

10 LaFrance Adrienne. 2020. "QAnon is More Important Than You Think." *The Atlantic.* https://www.theatlantic.com/magazine/archive/2020/06/qanon-nothing-can-stop-what-is-coming/610567/

11 Hayes, David. 2019. "The Coming Global Tsunami." *Praying Medic.* https://prayingmedic.com/2019/11/08/the-coming-global-tsunami/

12 Burgis, Ben and Wynn, Natalie. "GTAA Episode 17: Contrapoints." *Give Them an Argument.* https://www.youtube.com/watch?v=Fb6uR-4vcmA

13 Horkheimer, Max and Adorno, Theodor, p150. *The Dialectic of Enlightenment.* Stanford University Press, 2002.

14 Horkheimer, Max and Adorno, Theodor, p152. As above.

15 Horkheimer, Max and Adorno, Theodor, p159. As above.

16 Horkheimer, Max and Adorno, Theodor, p153. As above.

17 Editorial. 2020. "Why Are Witches Hexing the Moon on TikTok?" *New Scientist.* https://www.newscientist.com/article/mg24732941-300-why-are-witches-hexing-the-moon-on-tiktok/

18 https://twitter.com/marwilliamson/status/1285239347248336897?lang=en

19 Adorno, Theodor, p238. "Minima Moralia." Verso, 2005.

20 Fisher, Mark, p3. *Capitalist Realism: Is There No Alternative?* Zero Books, 2009.

21 Fisher, Mark, p2. As above.

22 Fisher, Mark, p3. As above.

23 Kiberd, Roisin. 2015. "The Rise and Fall of 'Boring Dystopia,' the Anti-Facebook Facebook Group." *Vice.* https://www.vice.com/en/article/aekd5j/the-rise-and-fall-of-boring-dystopia-the-anti-Facebook-Facebook-group

24 As above.

25 The "Minus the Shooting" blog can still be found here: http://minus-the-shooting.blogspot.com/

26 Adorno, Theodor, p140. *Minima Moralia.* Verso, 2005.

27 Adorno, Theory, p119. *Aesthetic Theory.* Continuum, 1997.

28 Fisher, Mark, p80. *Capitalist Realism: Is There No Alternative?* Zero Books, 2009.

29 Fisher, Mark, p9. As above.

30 Adorno, Theodor, p15. *Minima Moralia.* Verso, 2005.

31 A contextualization of this quote can be found in this blog article by Stuart Jeffries: https://www.versobooks.com/blogs/2791-the-storm-blowing-from-paradise-walter-benjamin-and-klee-s-angelus-novus

32 This wiki entry can be found here: https://knowyourmeme.com/memes/what-vibe-do-i-give-offhttps://knowyourmeme.com/memes/what-vibe-do-i-give-off

33 This description was personally related by Buck-Morss to Derek Bunyard who in turn recalled it in a lecture that can be read here: http://www.leeds.ac.uk/educol/

documents/00001879.htm The extent to which Buck-Morss sees Benjamin's method as reliant on shock can be seen in *The Dialectics of Seeing: Walter Benjamin and The Arcades Project*. MIT Press, 1989. See, for example, p219: "Benjamin was counting on the shock of this recognition to jolt the dreaming collective into a political awakening."

34 Sholem, Gerhard and Adorno, Theodor, Editors, pp494-503. *The Correspondence of Walter Benjamin*. University of Chicago Press, 2012.

35 Sholem, Gerhard and Adorno, Theodor, p495. As above.

36 Benjamin, Walter, p13. *The Arcades Project*. Harvard University Press, 2002.

37 Sholem, Gerhard and Adorno, Theodor, Editors, pp582-583. *The Correspondence of Walter Benjamin*. University of Chicago Press, 2012.

38 Benjamin, Walter, p422. *The Arcades Project*. Harvard University Press, 2002. Benjamin cites this craze for tortoises five times in *The Arcades Project*, linking the act of tortoise walking to the "rhythmics of slumber" on p106, signaling an induced lassitude in the middle classes, similar to that described by Mark Fisher in relation to his college students in *Capitalist Realism*.

39 Benjamin, Walter, p13. As above.

40 "Virtual Futures," University of Warwick, 18-19 June 2011. The talk can be seen here: https://www.youtube.com/watch?v=8Bk0kkRPmjE&t

41 Benjamin, Walter, p427. *The Arcades Project*. Harvard University Press, 2002.

42 Benjamin, Walter, p69. As above.

43 Benjamin, Walter, p514. As above.

44 Jeffries, Stuart. 2017. "The Effect of the Whip: The Frankfurt School and the Oppression of Women." *Verso Blog*. https://www.versobooks.com/blogs/2846-the-effect-of-the-whip-the-frankfurt-school-and-the-oppression-of-women

45 Horkheimer, Max and Adorno, Theodor, p112. *Dialectic of Enlightenment*. Stanford University Press, 2002.

46 Marcuse, Herbert, p77. *One Dimensional Man*. Routledge, 1991.

47 Marcuse, Herbert, p76. As above.

48 Marcuse, Herbert, p10. As above.

49 Marcuse, Herbert, p81. As above.

50 This wiki entry can be found here: https://knowyourmeme. com/memes/are-ya-winning-son

51 Marcuse, Herbert, p260. As above.

52 Marcuse, Herbert, pp260-261. As above.

53 Marcuse, Herbert, pp243. As above.

54 Marcuse, Herbert, pp67. As above.

55 Adorno, Theodor and Marcuse, Herbert. pp123-126. "Correspondence on the German student movement." *New Left Review*.

56 Adorno, Theodor and Marcuse, Herbert. As above.

57 Adorno, Theodor and Marcuse, Herbert. As above.

58 Adorno, Theodor and Marcuse, Herbert. As above.

59 The "breast action" happening as relayed in Der Spiegel, No. 19/1969 was recently revisited in Der Spiegel in 2020 by Hauke Goos: https://www.spiegel.de/kultur/literatur/ theodor-w-adorno-und-das-busenattentat-schoener- schreiben-die-deutschkolumne-a-1614d5b6-08c7-4118-859f- c2be34b24a1b

60 Marcuse, Herbert, p69. *The Aesthetic Dimension: Toward a Critique of Marxist Aesthetics*. Beacon Press, 1978.

61 Fisher, Mark. "Acid Communism." Kindle Edition: *K-Punk: The Collected and Unpublished Writings of Mark Fisher (2004-2016)*. Repeater, 2018.

62 Fisher, Mark. "Acid Communism." Kindle Edition: *K-Punk: The Collected and Unpublished Writings of Mark Fisher (2004-2016)*. Repeater, 2018.

References

Adorno, Theodor. *Aesthetic Theory*. Continuum, 1997.

Adorno, Theodor and Horkheimer, Max. *Dialectic of Enlightenment*. Stanford University Press, 2002.

Adorno, Theodor. *Minima Moralia*. Verso, 2005.

Attali, Jacques. *Noise: The Political Economy of Music*. Manchester University Press, 1985.

Benjamin, Walter. and Arendt, Hannah. *Illuminations*. Schocken Books, 1969.

Benjamin, Walter, p427. *The Arcades Project*. Harvard University Press, 2002.

Buck-Morss, Susan. *Dialectics of Seeing: Walter Benjamin and the Arcades Project*. MIT Press, 1989.

Fisher, Mark. *Capitalist Realism: Is There no Alternative?* Zero Books, 2009.

Fisher, Mark. *Ghosts of My Life: Writings on Depression, Hauntology and Lost Futures*. Zero Books, 2014.

Fisher, Mark. *K-Punk: The Collected and Unpublished Writings of Mark Fisher (2004-2016)*. Repeater, 2018. Kindle Edition.

Good, Hauke. *Das "Busenattentat" und ein Adorno-Moment*. Das Spiegel, 2020.

Hayes, David. *The Coming Global Tsunami*. Praying Medic, 2019.

Jeffries, Stuart. *The Storm Blowing from Paradise: Walter Benjamin and Paul Klee's Angelus Novus*. Verso Blog, 2016.

Jeffries, Stuart. *The Effect of the Whip: The Frankfurt School and the Oppression of Women*. Verso Blog, 2017.

Kiberd, Roisin. *The Rise and Fall of 'Boring Dystopia,' the Anti-Facebook Facebook Group*. Vice, 2015.

LaFrance, Adrienne. *QAnon is More Important Than You Think*. The Atlantic, 2020.

Marcuse, Herbert. *One Dimensional Man: Studies in the Ideology of Advanced Industrial Society*. Routledge, 2013.

Marcuse, Herbert. *Aesthetic Dimension*. Macmillan International Higher Education, 1979.

Sholem, Gerhard and Adorno, Theodor, Editors. *The Correspondence of Walter Benjamin*. University of Chicago Press, 2012.

Sontag, Susan. *On Photography*. Penguin, 2001.

CULTURE, SOCIETY & POLITICS

The modern world is at an impasse. Disasters scroll across our
smartphone screens and we're invited to like, follow or upvote,
but critical thinking is harder and harder to find. Rather than
connecting us in common struggle and debate, the internet has
sped up and deepened a long-standing process of alienation and
atomization. Zer0 Books wants to work against this trend.
With critical theory as our jumping off point, we aim to publish
books that make our readers uncomfortable. We want to move
beyond received opinions.
Zer0 Books is on the left and wants to reinvent the left. We are
sick of the injustice, the suffering and the stupidity that defines
both our political and cultural world, and we aim to find a new
foundation for a new struggle.

If this book has helped you to clarify an idea, solve a problem or
extend your knowledge, you may want to check out our online
content as well. Look for Zer0 Books: Advancing Conversations
in the iTunes directory and for our Zer0 Books YouTube channel.

Popular videos include:

Žižek and the Double Blackmain

The Intellectual Dark Web is a Bad Sign

Can there be an Anti-SJW Left?

Answering Jordan Peterson on Marxism

Follow us on Facebook
at https://www.facebook.com/ZeroBooks and Twitter at https://
twitter.com/Zer0Books

Bestsellers from Zer0 Books include:

Give Them An Argument
Logic for the Left
Ben Burgis
Many serious leftists have learned to distrust talk of logic. This is
a serious mistake.
Paperback: 978-1-78904-210-8 ebook: 978-1-78904-211-5

Poor but Sexy
Culture Clashes in Europe East and West
Agata Pyzik
How the East stayed East and the West stayed West.
Paperback: 978-1-78099-394-2 ebook: 978-1-78099-395-9

An Anthropology of Nothing in Particular
Martin Demant Frederiksen
A journey into the social lives of meaninglessness.
Paperback: 978-1-78535-699-5 ebook: 978-1-78535-700-8

In the Dust of This Planet
Horror of Philosophy vol. 1
Eugene Thacker
In the first of a series of three books on the Horror of Philosophy,
In the Dust of This Planet offers the genre of horror as a way of
thinking about the unthinkable.
Paperback: 978-1-84694-676-9 ebook: 978-1-78099-010-1

The End of Oulipo?
An Attempt to Exhaust a Movement
Lauren Elkin, Veronica Esposito
Paperback: 978-1-78099-655-4 ebook: 978-1-78099-656-1

Capitalist Realism
Is There No Alternative?
Mark Fisher
An analysis of the ways in which capitalism has presented itself
as the only realistic political-economic system.
Paperback: 978-1-84694-317-1 ebook: 978-1-78099-734-6

Rebel Rebel
Chris O'Leary
David Bowie: every single song. Everything you want to know,
everything you didn't know.
Paperback: 978-1-78099-244-0 ebook: 978-1-78099-713-1

Kill All Normies
Angela Nagle
Online culture wars from 4chan and Tumblr to Trump.
Paperback: 978-1-78535-543-1 ebook: 978-1-78535-544-8

Cartographies of the Absolute
Alberto Toscano, Jeff Kinkle
An aesthetics of the economy for the twenty-first century.
Paperback: 978-1-78099-275-4 ebook: 978-1-78279-973-3

Malign Velocities
Accelerationism and Capitalism
Benjamin Noys
Long listed for the Bread and Roses Prize 2015, *Malign Velocities*
argues against the need for speed, tracking acceleration
as the symptom of the ongoing crises of capitalism.
Paperback: 978-1-78279-300-7 ebook: 978-1-78279-299-4

Meat Market
Female Flesh under Capitalism
Laurie Penny
A feminist dissection of women's bodies as the fleshy fulcrum of
capitalist cannibalism, whereby women are both consumers and
consumed.
Paperback: 978-1-84694-521-2 ebook: 978-1-84694-782-7

Babbling Corpse
Vaporwave and the Commodification of Ghosts
Grafton Tanner
Paperback: 978-1-78279-759-3 ebook: 978-1-78279-760-9

New Work New Culture
Work we want and a culture that strengthens us
Frithjof Bergmann
A serious alternative for mankind and the planet.
Paperback: 978-1-78904-064-7 ebook: 978-1-78904-065-4

Digesting Recipes
The Art of Culinary Notation
Susannah Worth
A recipe is an instruction, the imperative tone of the expert, but
this constraint can offer its own kind of potential. A recipe need
not be a domestic trap but might instead offer escape – something
to fantasise about or aspire to.
Paperback: 978-1-78279-860-6 ebook: 978-1-78279-859-0

Most titles are published in paperback and as an ebook.
Paperbacks are available in traditional bookshops. Both print and
ebook formats are available online.
Follow us on Facebook
at https://www.facebook.com/ZeroBooks
and Twitter at https://twitter.com/Zer0Books